THE
ELITE
CONSENSUS
WHEN CORPORATIONS WIELD THE CONSTITUTION

THE ELITE CONSENSUS

WHEN CORPORATIONS WIELD THE CONSTITUTION

By George Draffan

With a foreword by
Richard L. Grossman
and Ward Morehouse

POCLAD PROGRAM ON CORPORATIONS,
LAW AND DEMOCRACY

 THE APEX PRESS, NEW YORK

The Program on Corporations, Law and Democracy (POCLAD) was created in 1995 to instigate conversations and actions that contest the authority of corporations to define our culture, govern our nation, and plunder the Earth. Seeking to strengthen institutions that disperse, rather than concentrate, wealth and power, we work to fulfill the democratic ideals of the Declaration of Independence and the American Revolution.

Engage us at P.O. Box 246, South Yarmouth, MA 02664

people@poclad.org │ www.poclad.org │ phone 508.398.1145

Published by The Apex Press for The Program on Corporations, Law and Democracy (POCLAD). The Apex Press, an imprint of the Council on International and Public Affairs, is located at 777 United Nations Plaza, Suite 3C, New York, NY 10017.

Its publications office can be reached by telephone at 800.316.APEX (2739) or 914.271-6500, by mail at P.O. Box 337, Croton-on-Hudson, NY 10520 or by email at cipany@igc.org. Visit The Apex Press online at www.cipa-apex.org.

An earlier version of this book was published as *The Corporate Consensus: A Guide to the Institutions of Global Power,* by the Blue Mountains Biodiversity Project (HCR 82, Fossil, OR 97830) in October 2000.

Library of Congress Cataloging-in-Publication Data
Draffan, George, 1954-
The elite consensus: when corporations wield the Constitution/by George Draffan ; with foreword by Richard L. Grossman and Ward Morehouse.
p. cm.
ISBN 1-891843-14-1 (pbk.)
1. Business and politics—United States.
2. Corporations—United States—Political activity.
3. Corporation law—United States.
4. Constitutional law—United States
I. Title
JK467.D73 2003
322'.3'0973—dc21   2003041473

Printed in the United States of America by Thomson-Shore, Inc., an employee owned company, with soy inks on recycled paper.

Corporation: an ingenious device for obtaining individual profit without individual responsibility.

Journalist Ambrose Bierce[1]

I see in the near future a crisis approaching that unnerves me and causes me to tremble for the safety of my country. . . . Corporations have been enthroned and an era of corruption in high places will follow; and the money power of the country will endeavor to prolong its reign by working upon the prejudices of the people until all wealth is aggregated in a few hands and the Republic is destroyed.

U.S. President Abraham Lincoln[2]

If small business goes, big business does not have any future except to become the economic arm of a totalitarian state.

General Electric CEO Philip D. Reed[3]

Capitalism is the greatest thing going, but unchecked it is its own undoing.

*U.S. Securities & Exchange Commission
enforcement director Stanley Sporkin*[4]

Don't try to reform the current system. It is hopeless. It is impossible.

U.S. Speaker of the House Newt Gingrich[5]

[1] Bierce lampooned politicians and raked corporate muck for various newspapers and magazines, including those of William Randolph Hearst. Bierce disappeared in Mexico during the Revolution. Bierce's classic, *The Devil's Dictionary* defines, impunity as "wealth."

[2] From a November 21, 1864 letter to Colonel William F. Elkins, quoted in *The Lincoln Encyclopedia*. Lincoln, a railroad attorney before his election, did his part to bring on the corporations. In the 1860 Presidential election campaign, Lincoln's opponent Stephen Douglas spent $50,000; Lincoln spent $100,000. Once President, Lincoln, who saw that a national infrastructure was crucial to industrial progress, presided over the transfer of millions of acres of public land to railroad corporations *(see the Railroads & Clearcuts website at www.landgrant.org)*. See also Richard Hofstadter, Abraham Lincoln and the Self-Made Myth, in *The American Political Tradition* (Vintage, 1973).

[3] Reed was chairman of General Electric (1939-59) and of the Federal Reserve Bank of New York (1959-65), and active in the Council on Foreign Relations and other organizations.

[4] Quoted in *New York Times Magazine*, Sept. 26, 1976. Sporkin spent twenty years at the SEC; when Ronald Reagan appointed SEC chairman William Casey as director of the CIA, Sporkin began five years as the CIA's general counsel; Sporkin issued the legal finding that provided cover for the Reagan Administration's arms-for-hostages deal with Iran. Sporkin was appointed a U.S. District Court judge in 1986, and has been called by Ralph Nader "a rare judge who is sympathetic to the way the law intersects with consumer interests and investor interests." Sporkin ruled against Exxon's initial Alaskan oil spill settlement, and against banker Charles Keating's attempt to get back Lincoln Savings after it was seized by the government — but many observers predict that Sporkin's rulings in the anti-trust trial of Microsoft will be overruled. See Richard Lacayo, The Judge Who Makes Everything His Business, *Time,* Feb 27, 1994; and David Einstein, The Judge Who Rejected Microsoft, *San Francisco Chronicle,* Feb 16, 1995, p. D1.

[5] Quoted in Andy Pasztor, *When the Pentagon Was for Sale: Inside America's Biggest Defense Scandal* (Scribner, 1995), p. 367. Gingrich served twenty years in Congress. In 1994 he led Republican opposition against the Clinton Administration and orchestrated the "Contract With America." In 1995 he became Speaker of the House. In 1996, a House Ethics Commitee probe centered on Gingrich's use of charitable organizations to subsidize partisan political activities, and in 1997, the House voted overwhelmingly to reprimand Gingrich and ordered him to pay a $300,000 penalty — "the first time in the House's 208-year history it has disciplined a speaker for ethical wrongdoing." Gingrich resigned from Congress in 1998, but has been busy since, generating non-profit oganizations for his partisan political activities. See Charles R. Babcock, Use of Tax-Exempt Groups Integral to Political Strategy, *Washington Post,* Jan 7, 1997, p. A1; and John E. Yang, House Reprimands, Penalizes Speaker, *Washington Post,* Jan 22, 1997, p. A1.

ACKNOWLEDGEMENTS

The author would like to thank Karen Coulter of the Blue Mountains Biodiversity Project for conceiving of and implementing this project. Her love of the natural world is matched only by her determination to stop the destruction and injustice wrought by corporate power.

Funding for various pieces of the research, writing, publishing and distributing of this book has been provided by the McKenzie River Gathering Foundation, the Foundation for Deep Ecology and Resist Illegitimate Authority, Inc. While their support made this project possible, none of them are responsible for the contents or conclusions of this book.

Helpful suggestions and comments on early drafts of the book were provided by Aziz Choudry, Radha D'Souza, Jeffrey Kaplan and Janine Blaeloch, each of them an extraordinary activist against corporate power. Paulette Pollard skillfully edited a mass of material into the introductory survey of corporate power.

Thanks to Matt Wuerker for the cover illustration. He can be contacted at *mcwuerker@yahoo.com*.

The author's website at www.endgame.org includes A Primer on Corporate Power, a Directory of Transnational Corporations, several Activist Research Manuals, a Clearinghouse on Forests and Corporations, links to many research sources and activist groups and information on workshops and seminars on corporate power.

TABLE OF CONTENTS

The 1st Amendment "does not intend to guarantee men freedom to say what some private interest pays them to say for its own advantage. It intends only to make men free to say what, as citizens, they think."

Alexander Meiklejohn
Philosopher & Educator (1872-1964)

FOREWORD

"Over the past 200 years, all over the world but especially in the United States, legal systems have been changed to accomplish two things: limit the legal liabilities of corporations, and give corporations the rights and protections of citizens" by extending "constitutional rights to corporations." So writes George Draffan in this book about the few who govern the many.

These two accomplishments have enabled corporate officers "to make decisions and control resources . . . to unite to influence political agendas" towards transforming their values and goals (maximizing production, paying as few workers as possible as little as possible, building complex industrial systems, propelling America as Empire, etc.) into law and policy.

What does this mean for all the people hired and fired at will by corporate managers? For people who value cooperation, love, human rights, ecological sanity, democracy and consent of the governed? It means that a unified corporate class uses the law of the land to deny the majority's fundamental right to govern.

It means that a relatively small number of corporate operatives use "the rule of law" to keep millions and millions of people divided and disempowered.

Routine corporate decisions involving investment, labor and the natural world cause so much harm to life, liberty and property that millions struggle to figure out which corporation is doing what to whom. They scrutinize each new corporate technology, corporate merger, and proposed corporate law; study finance and interlocking corporate structures. Millions have become experts on water, forests, soils, climate; have learned chemistry, physics, hydrology, biology and finance; have learned how to make their way through regulatory and administrative agencies.

Time and again people have come together to oppose corporate plans. They have declared: Not In Our Names. Not Here. Not There. Not Anywhere. This civic work has been vital—to save life and land, to lift the human spirit, to teach children. But while people were resisting corporate assaults and working for sane investments and technologies, corporate operatives were making the rules for governing the nation.

So people are saying "No" in ways which challenge corporate claims to constitutional authority; which reveal the histories of slave owner—and then corporation owner—usurpations; which confront public officials with trampling upon people's basic rights.

George advances this exciting evolution as he dissects the elite consensus—"larger than any industry"—relentlessly pitching its manufactured histories, destructive values, false choices and global empire; aggressively selling and reselling ever-more production of everything possible as the fount of liberty.

He reveals the motivation driving this corporate consensus that "rises above the competitive advantage of particular corporations, and is larger than any industry." It is "to build and maintain power itself." To thwart democracy. To govern the Earth.

Today's corporate leaders received a head start from the men of property who wrote the Constitution.

When the overwhelmingly white male voters of the thirteen states ratified the Constitution, the "rule of law" they adopted defined the majority of human beings in those states as property, or as invisible. Contrary to the democratic ideals unleashed by the American Revolution, the law in this newly-formed republic denied rights to women, African American slaves, indentured servants, Native peoples, and white males without property.

All these human beings were written out of "We the people."

Who represented their needs and aspirations? Not the men meeting behind closed doors in Philadelphia's Constitution Hall that hot summer of 1787. These men not only denied rights to the majority but also built barriers to democratic processes into their Constitution: indirect election of the president through the electoral college, indirect election of US senators by state legislators, a commerce clause, a contracts clause, an appointed Supreme Court as an eternal closed-door constitutional convention,[1] to name a few.

The Revolutionary Era's propertied and slave-owning gentlemen who wrote the Constitution used law to keep the histories, experiences, needs, values and aspirations of the denied from being transformed into public policy. Parading their stolen powers as "constitutional rights," they provided future elites with the "legal" means to expand their rule even after whole classes of people had won the right to vote, to run for public office, to own property, to speak, to go to school, to form unions, to serve on juries and testify in court, to enjoy public accommodations, etc.

Since Southern slaveowners and northern men of property controlled the mechanisms of governance in the nation's early years, they saw no need to muscle up the corporation—a tool of kings with which they had direct experience. These men who were doing very well did not want rival ruling power controlled by others, like the East India Company, to arise in their midst. So their state legislators wrote corporate charters—and then state corporation laws—limiting how long corporations could exist and limiting their real property and capital holdings. Laws in all states specified corporate purpose, banned corporations from owning other corporations, preserved rights of minority shareholders, made directors and shareholders liable for corporate debts and harms, and barred corporate involvement in elections and lobbying.

The culture regarded corporations as subordinate to the sovereign people.

After the Civil War, however, the men setting out to industrialize this land with machines and workers without rights made the corporation their ruling institution. As men of property had wrapped the Constitution around themselves in 1787, men of the Gilded Age enlisted judges and legislators to wrap the nation's sacred text around their new financial and industrial conglomerates.

By the end of the 19th Century, corporations had been baptized in the contract, commerce, property and personhood pools the Revolutionary elite had dammed into the Constitution one hundred years before. Public officials in New Jersey, and then Delaware, lay down for Rockefeller's Standard Oil Corporation, for the DuPont family and for men of great wealth controlling everything from food to steel to matches to armaments to whiskey. Robber barons began buying up other corporations, using them to create *even more* corporations swaddled in the Constitution.

A century later, corporate lobbying and propaganda think tanks, charities, foundations and other corporate clones masquerade as We the People. They sport goodness and mercy monikers like "Patriotic Citizens for Secure Jobs and All-American Energy" and "Good Neighbors for Fair and Democratic Chemicals." On talk shows; in op-ed pages; in seances with elected officials in governors' offices, legislatures and judges' chambers; at meetings of the World Trade Organization and the United Nations; at international conferences; and in endless advertisements, corporate shills say what they are paid to say.

They tell governments what to do.

Wielding such power generation after generation breeds a special arrogance. Consider this: a few years ago, leaders of Travelers Group and Citibank corporations decided to merge. There was one minor problem: such a merger was against the law. But confident that in no time they could pass a new law wiping out a fifty-year old law, they went full speed ahead.

Their confidence was justified. A New York Times Corporation photograph adorning our POCLAD walls captures a blissed-out elite consensus moment at the White House. The caption reads:

> "Depression-Era Rules Undone. Alan Greenspan, left, the Federal Reserve Chairman, and Congressional leaders applauded President Clinton yesterday after he signed the Financial Services Modernization Act, which allows merging of banks, securities firms and insurers. It repeals parts of the Glass-Steagall Act."

Why do corporations get away with it? Because with few exceptions, civic activists have not looked closely at this history. They have not contested the nation's corporate class over its grab of governing authority.[2] So let's look more closely at how the nation got into this mess.

Until the Civil War, political power was held primarily by the representatives of large slave holders like George Washington, Thomas Jefferson and James Madison, who used their domination of southern state governments to direct the United States government. The constitution that they wrote guaranteed profits from the new government's denial of human rights by, among other things, directing government to guarantee the return of all "persons held to service or labor in one State"[3] to their rightful owners. ("Persons" here meant both African American slaves and white slaves better known today as indentured servants.) The Constitution provided as well that the armed might of the United States would aid states against rebellions (called "domestic violence"[4]) by workers—whether they were chattel slaves or wage slaves.

Their Constitution also decreed their domination of politics and lawmaking. A slave was to count as "3/5 of a person"[5] for assigning representation in the House of Representatives and the Electoral College. This meant that slave state elites could turn their ownership of human beings into domination over congressional and presidential elections.[6]

The rise of northern industrialists after the Civil War brought the end of slave master rule and the beginning of rule by corporate kings. As happened after the Revolution had been won, Southern and Northern men of property again united. They wrote slavery out of the Constitution with the "Civil War Amendments,"[7] and wrote corporations in. Industrialists then used government to defeat organized resistance by women, former slaves, farmers, workers and small businessmen seeking to reconstruct the nation as a democracy based on free labor and equal rights. They did the same to Native peoples seeking to preserve their independence.

These elites stole the presidential election of 1876.[8] They then established "new trends in legal doctrine and political-economic theory" to enable "the corporate reorganization of the property-production system."[9]

After ratification of the 13th, 14th and 15th amendments, judges and legislators concocted constitutional doctrines legalizing racial segregation and exploitation,[10] and denial of workers' rights no matter the worker's race, creed, gender or color.[11] As a result, men of property could call upon sheriffs, militias, police, jails and courts to enforce Jim Crow, anti-free labor, anti-union, anti-strike, conspiracy and sedition laws at local, state and national levels. They directed the coercive force of law—legalized violence—to prevent the majority from using elections, lawmaking and lawsuits to remedy harms or pass the laws they wanted.

Over succeeding generations they directed government force and violence to deny African Americans, Native peoples, Asians, women, immigrants from the global south, war resisters—anyone spouting anti-elite values—their most fundamental rights.

These industrialists were simply acting in an old tradition. After all, the forebears of the new corporate class had written a constitution trashing the Declaration of Independence's "all men are created equal; that they are endowed by their Creator with certain unalienable Rights; that among these are Life, Liberty, and the pursuit of Happiness. That to secure these right, Governments are instituted among Men, deriving their just powers from the consent of the governed . . ."

So for more than two centuries, the nation's elite minority has arrayed government against the assembling, speaking out and petitioning by African Americans, enslaved and free; by working people and their unions; by Native peoples and immigrants; by family farmers and small businesspeople. They have arrayed government against people whose lands and labor they desired; or whose appearance, thoughts, speech, assembling and governing they feared.[12]

They did this despite the plain and simple language of the Constitution's very first amendment: "Congress shall make no law . . . abridging the freedom of speech, or of the press; or the right of the people peaceably to assemble, and to petition the Government for a redress of grievances."

Since 1868, they did this despite the plain and simple language of the 14th amendment: ". . . No State shall make or enforce any law which shall abridge the privileges or immunities of citizens of the United States; nor shall any State deprive any person of life, liberty or property, without due process of law; nor deny to any person within its jurisdiction the equal protection of the laws."

They did all this without writing the words "slave," or "segregation," or "labor union," or "foreigner," or "un-American," or "separate but equal," into the nation's plan of governance. While raving about "democracy," "liberty," "freedom." While making gods of the "Founding Fathers."

Now that's wielding the Constitution!

There is another word which does not appear in the Constitution — "corporation."

Men of property have had no difficulty encouraging Supreme Court justices to find corporations in the nation's sacred text. Beginning with the 1819 Dartmouth College case[13], judges bestowed the privileges upon corporations which white, male, propertied human persons had already seized for themselves. This, of course, meant the denial of *everyone else's* rights.

During railway workers' 1894 strike against the Pullman Corporation, the justices upheld local judges who had banned American Railway Union officials from speaking with members and had thrown union leaders in jail. For a unanimous Court, Justice David Brewer declared: ". . . the army of the Nation, and all its militia, are at the service of the Nation to compel obedience to its laws."[14]

This is not the language justices used when human persons petitioned them for redress of grievances. (See, for example, Dred Scott,[15] Plessy,[16] Minor,[17] Mackay,[18] Brown,[19] and hundreds of Supreme Court decisions).

On the contrary: judges decreed that corporations could brandish those "due process of law" and "equal protection of the laws" powers of the 14th Amendment and the "due process" clause of the 5th Amendment. They expanded corporations' commerce, contract and other constitutional authority. In so doing, they barred municipal, state and congressional legislation making the economy subject to public law, or directing government power to kick corporations out of village squares, elections, government halls, judges' chambers and the Constitution.

Since World War II, judicial gifts of 1st Amendment powers to corporations have continued undermining the ability of voters to instruct elected legislators. As Professor Mark Tushnet observed: "The 1st amendment has replaced the due process clause as the primary guarantor of the privileged. Indeed, it protects the privileged more perniciously than the due process clause ever did . . ."[20]

Today, corporate directors and their non-profit corporations straddle the twin pillars of the 14th and 1st amendments, as Matt Wuerker portrays on the cover of this book. Unleashing their intellectuals, propagandists and lobbyists for hire, buying the loyalty of or silencing community groups, schools and the press (including public radio and public television), they drive the nation's debate, values, investments, technologies, legal relationships and wars.

Non-profit corporate creations of today's elites subvert people's ability to "secure the blessings of liberty to ourselves and our posterity."[21] They shut people up and out of any decisionmaking which counts. Their Supreme Court nullifies any people's laws which even minimally challenge corporate authority.[22]

The majority of people in these United States are constitutionally disabled.

No wonder people are exhausted and disillusioned from forays into campaign finance reform, corporate responsibility, EPA, NLRB, SEC, NRC, FDA, FCC and other corporate regulatory struggles. No wonder there is so much cultural pressure on communities, concerned citizens — and even academics and public interest lawyers — against linking people's multiple single-issues struggles against corporate assaults. No wonder that people are instructed over and over again (often by many leaders of environmental, human rights and labor groups) that we must not aspire to anything more than begging for "acceptable" levels of corporate class lobbying, election domination, wage enslavement and Earthly poisoning.

No wonder people are rethinking their work in this corporate world. Enter George Draffan and *The Elite Consensus*.

In this book George examines "institutions which support corporate power" from the World Bank, the International Monetary Fund and the World Trade Organization to the Council on Foreign Relations, the Cato Institute, NATO and the United Nations. He includes public relations and advertising corporations into which elites pour hundreds of billions of tax-deductible[23] dollars . . . along with corporate propagandists posing as journalists and pundits.

George shows how a few people shape ideas, policies, values, news, information and language while writing laws and rewriting histories. He makes clear that by the time "issues" or even honest candidates appear before the voters, they have been sterilized, sanitized, disinfected and fumigated to order by the elite consensus.

By *that* time, intellectuals at corporate think tanks have done their trashy-but-footnoted studies and reports. By that time, journalists, editors, TV news writers, public officials and community leaders have been properly educated. Peoples' energies have been channeled into Potemkin Villages propped up by corporate fairy tales and democratic myths, as depicted in Matt Wuerker's cover.

Shill corporations like the Cato Institute, the Chamber of Commerce, the Business Roundtable and the Heritage Foundation have spent years and billions of dollars fabricating idea deconstruction systems constantly spewing cockamamie that frames and reframes and reframes the country's agendas. Their managing of the nation's discussions can be seen in the ways Social Security, fast track legislation, global rights agreements like NAFTA, war in the Middle East, energy and health care policies, revelations of corporate usurpations and other issues in the news are mass-produced from coast to coast.

Encouraging people to deny their own experiences and crushing people's aspirations — that's power. Using police, militias, courts and jails to limit people's ability to exercise rights collectively (such as speech and assembly) they cannot exercise as individuals — that's mastery.

George's first chapter, "Cultural Power: The Colonization of Our Minds," looks at how mass media, PR and other corporate foundations, think tanks and lobby groups do this work.

Chapter two probes the corporate use of the "rule of law" as a means of "leveraging authority." The third chapter focuses on the reality that so many industries and services are oligopolies dominated by a few corporate conglomerates wealthier than most nations.

Next, George looks at the iron fist inside the PR-camouflaged corporate glove. He helps us remember that even when huge groups of people challenged governance by corporations, public officials responded with violence.

Haven't demonstrators against global corporatization and war — from Seattle to Los Angeles, Philadelphia, Washington DC and smaller communities — found our own government arrayed against them wrapped in the uniform of Ninja warriors?

The second part of *The Elite Consensus* profiles leading terrorist corporations—such as the Chamber of Commerce, the Trilateral Commission, the Council on Foreign Relations. George provides useful information about the origins, budgets, directors and work of each. We learn, for instance, that Defense Secretary Donald Rumsfeld was a director of the Hoover Institution (which had placed many of its members in the Reagan administration). So was David Packard of "military and electronics giant" Hewlett-Packard Corporation. We see that in the mid-1990s, National Public Radio correspondent Anne Garrels spent two years in Russia as a "fellow with the Council on Foreign Relations."

A decade ago, 79 of the Business Roundtable's directors "held 206 board seats in 134 corporations." In 1999 the Brookings Institution had $225 million in net assets. Petroleum corporation millionaires David and Charles Koch fund not only the Cato Institute but also Citizens for a Sound Economy. Among the directors of that group have been C. Boyden Gray (former counsel to George H. W. Bush) and James C. Miller III (former director of the Office of Management and Budget and chair of the Federal Trade Commission).

As icing on the cake, George offers eight appendices documenting selected dynamics of corporate power. He ranks corporate expenditures for writing laws, links top lobbyists with their corporate clients, follows the flow of corporate money as it violates the body politic, and summarizes studies examining creative corporate extractions of public funds.

These corporate profiles bring the elite consensus to life![24]

The Elite Consensus reveals how a propertied class which long ago figured out how to write—and keep on writing—the Constitution kills democratic thought, nips democratic institutions in the bud and diverts organizing for democratic self-governance, over and over again. George's analysis complements the work and publications of the Program on Corporations, Law & Democracy described at the end of this volume. POCLAD is pleased to join with The Apex Press to bring you this new edition of George's book.

Richard L. Grossman and Ward Morehouse
Co-Founders, Program On Corporations,
Law & Democracy (POCLAD)
November 2002

[1] As Justice Robert Jackson said of this august body: "We are not final because we are infallible, but we are infallible only because we are final." Brown v Allen, 344 US 443, 540 (1953).

[2] Since the great corporate-imposed un-American scare following World War II, and the government repression of thought, speech, assembly and civic action it spawned, corporate leaders have been far more conscious about strengthening their *governing* role than have been most of their critics. In the 1970s, for example, they launched (and funded with millions of dollars) a non-profit corporate attack group called "Americans Against Union Control of Government," a "subsidiary" of the National Right to Work Committee. As Gerald Colby described, "Like the Liberty Lobby of the 1930s, these groups served as a front for DuPont and other large corporations..." *DuPont Dynasty*, Secaucus NJ: Lyle Stewart Inc., (1984), p. 750. As far as we know, there has never been a people's group with a name like "Americans Against Corporate Control of Government." Only in the past few years have contemporary activists defending against corporate assaults begun to grapple with the reality that corporations *govern the nation enabled and protected by the rule of law... by the Constitution.*

[3] Article IV, section 2, part 3.

[4] Article IV, Section 4.

[5] Article I, Section 3.

[6] In 28 of the nation's first 32 years, the president was from a slave state: Washington, Jefferson, Madison, and Monroe, each of whom served two terms in office, were from Virginia.

[7] The 13th Amendment, banning slavery and involuntary servitude, was ratified in 1865; the 14th amendment, defining "All persons born or naturalized in the US..." as citizens of the US, and declaring that no state shall "deprive any person of life, liberty or property, without due process of law," was ratified in 1868; the 15th amendment, declaring that the "right of citizens of the US to vote shall not be denied or abridged by the US or by any State on account of race, color, or previous condition of servitude," was ratified in 1870.

[8] See "Property Picks A President," by Mike Ferner, in *By What Authority,* volume 3, number 2, Spring 2001.

[9] Martin J. Sklar, *The Corporate Reconstruction of American Capitalism, 1890-1916, The Market, The Law and Politics,* NY: Cambridge University Press, 1988, p. 85.

[10] See, among many examples, *Plessy v. Ferguson,* 163 US 537 (1896).

[11] See, among many examples: *Topeka & Santa Fe Railway Corporation v Gee,* 139 F. 582, 584 (C. C. S. D. Iowa), (1905)— "[t]here is and can be no such thing as peaceful picketing, any more than there can be chaste vulgarity or peaceful mobbing, or lawful lynching. When men want to converse or persuade, they do not organize a picket line."

[12] See, among many examples: *Schenck v United States,* 249 US 47 (1919); *Whitney v California,* 274 US 357, 372 (1927).

[13] *Dartmouth College v Woodward,* 4 Wheat. 518 (1819). See "You've Heard of Santa Clara, Now Meet Dartmouth," by Peter Kellman, in *Defying*

Corporations, Defining Democracy, published for POCLAD by The Apex Press, 2001.

[14] *In Re: Debs*, 158 US 564 (1895).

[15] *Dred Scott v Sandford*, 19 How. 393 (1857).

[16] *Plessy v Ferguson*, 163 US 537, 16 S. Ct. 1138, 41 L. Ed. 256 (1896).

[17] *Minor v Happersett*, 88 US 162 (1875).

[18] *NLRB v Mackay Radio & Tel. Co.*, 304 US 333 (1938).

[19] *Brown v Board of Education*, 347 US 483, 74 S. Ct. 686, 98 L. Ed. 873 (1954).

[20] "An Essay on Rights," *Texas Law Review*, Vol. 62, 1984.

[21] From the Preamble to the Constitution of the United States.

[22] See among many, many Federal court decisions, e.g., George A. O'Toole of Federal District Court nullifying a Massachusetts "law requiring tobacco companies to list the ingredients of their products, saying it forces the companies to give away trade secrets," *NY Times*, 10 September 2000; nullification of a New Jersey law banning the transit of toxic waste through its borders, *Philadelphia v New Jersey*, 437 US 617 (1978).

[23] Law today defines corporate propaganda, along with lawyers' fees and a large proportion of executive salaries and expense accounts, and penalizing fines, as normal costs of business. These costs are tax-deductible . . . which means that We the People pay for much of our own manipulation.

[24] The Enron Corporation Saga shows that George is on the money. *The Nation* (29 January 2002), reports that Ken Lay financed a chair at the corporate think tank Resources For the Future (RFF), a creation of the Brookings Institution. "Lay's gift to RFF, according to the group's newsletter, was to underwrite research 'to improve the way decision-makers consider important issues on the top of the nation's policy agenda.'" *The Nation* also reveals that Lay was a "board member and funder of the conservative American Enterprise Institute."

INTRODUCTION

In the past century, the limited liability corporation became the most powerful institution in the world, both politically and economically—and increasingly on the cultural level as well. Corporations accumulate wealth and exercise power through alliances with other corporations and through relationships with local, national, and international government officials.

The World Trade Organization (WTO), with its explicit jurisdiction superceding national laws, has recently provided a focal point and raised the public's awareness of the concentration of political and economic power in the hands of fewer and fewer people. Multilateral financial institutions like the World Bank and International Monetary Fund, controlled by the richest nations, are privatizing the economies and restructuring the social policies of the rest of the world.

But the World Bank and the WTO are only the more visible institutions of corporate power. Government agencies charged with protecting public health and safety are run by executives on loan from the corporations that are supposed to be regulated. Corporate lobby groups write legislation and buy candidates for political office. Corporate-driven think tanks and educators enjoy the prestige of university appointments where corporate agendas are developed and disseminated. Corporate foundations decide which charities and which environmental groups will get funded. Investment bankers control more money than the World Bank, and their unregulated speculation in national currencies has plunged Latin America and Asia into financial crises. Governments have become "mere salesmen" promoting multinational corporations, which are the "muscle and brains" of the global economy.[1]

The purpose of this book is to help provide an understanding of the organizations that are most influential in economic and political decisions at the national and international levels. Individual corporations wield enormous influence over government policy-makers, communities, and entire regional economies, but the true measure of corporate power is the ability of the owners and managers of corporations to unite to influence political agendas and to subvert national and international law. Therefore the focus of this book is on the full range of institutions which support corporate power—including think tanks, policy groups, lobbying associations, trade bodies, and multilateral trade and development agencies—rather than on individual corporations *(see Appendix 4 for a list of the 500 largest corporations)*.[2]

Some institutions (the Business Roundtable, the Chamber of Commerce) have long been recognized as major corporate associations. Other organizations (the World Trade Organization, the European Roundtable of Industrialists) are relatively new on the scene, but are undeniably centers of corporate power and globalization. The inclusion of other institutions in this book (NATO, the United Nations) may come as a surprise to some readers, but the discussion will show that they too promote corporate power. Knowledge of these organizations is critical to understanding and addressing the sources of the environmental, economic, and social problems posed by corporate power.

The usefulness of this knowledge will depend on the kind of work activists do. Some activists will find it useful in helping the public understand how the political system works. They may wish to point out to people that their elected and appointed officials meet every year with corporate executives for a week of schmoozing and strategizing in Switzerland, or remind local journalists that U.S. Cabinet Secretaries are corporate executives who give government contracts to their business partners. Other activists may find the book useful in their efforts to change the way the trade policies are made, perhaps by focusing on the interlocks between the U.S. Trade Representative and his or her Industry Sector Advisory Committees, which are made up of representatives of major corporations. Activists who want to challenge corporate charters may wish to focus on corporations whose executives have also been leaders in the lobbying and policy organizations. A list of the world's largest corporations, and several lists of the leaders of corporate politics are included in the appendices.

Part 1 of this book surveys how economic, legal and political mechanisms work together to maintain corporate power. (An expanded version of this survey, with historical and modern case studies, is available on the author's website at *www.endgame.org*.) Part 2 profiles the most powerful lobbying, research and political organizations promoting corporate power.

1

THE DYNAMICS OF POWER

THE ANATOMY OF CORPORATE POWER

Activists seek to locate the "mechanisms" of power, but power is not a machine. Power, the ability to make decisions and control resources, is found in the dynamics of the relationships between people. Depending on how power flows and who wields it, political and economic decisions are made and resources flow between individuals, groups, and corporations. When society's economic, political, and social structures become institutionalized, power tends to flow from people into institutions, but not back again. Power becomes concentrated.

The flow of power to corporations is promoted by legal mechanisms such as corporate personhood, limits to liability, pollution permitting, and political campaign financing, and by institutional structures such as regulatory agencies, export credit agencies, and police forces and armies. Together, these mechanisms and structures maintain networks of tightly-held power. Network analysis has shown that ninety percent of the 800 largest U.S. corporations are interlocked in a continuous network, with any one corporation within four steps of any other corporation in the network.[3]

Analysis of think tanks and policy groups in the early 1990s showed that the Business Roundtable was interlocked most extensively, followed by the Business Council, the Conference Board, the Committee for Economic Development, Brookings Institution, American Enterprise Institute, Council on Foreign Relations, Trilateral Commission, Hoover Institution, Chamber of Commerce, and Heritage Foundation.[4] Some of these institutions are being displaced by new ones. Interlocks are not the only source of power, and in any case, the precise measurement of power is impossible. But the enormous influence of these and other global alliances of corporate power is undeniable.

Corporations and corporate foundations fund think tanks which formulate policies which will be favorable to business. Corporate attorneys draft legislation which will make those policies the law of the land. Corporate political action committees pay for the election campaigns of the politicians who ensure that such legislation becomes law, and lobbyists make sure the politicians stay bought. Corporate executives are appointed to lead the regulatory agencies which enforce (or dismantle) the laws that aren't favorable to business. National and multilateral trade and development agencies design and subsidize an international trading system dominated by the largest corporations. Governments and banks use public monies to subsidize and insure corporate investment.

The elite consensus rises above the competitive advantage of particular corporations, and is larger than any industry. What unites corporations and industry associations and the wealthy and powerful is a consensus to build and maintain power itself. Corporate power is dependent on legal, economic, and political mechanisms, structures, and processes which follow a few basic rules:

- *Privatize profits.* Get as many subsidies as possible from labor, the public, and the environment. Get below-cost raw materials from the public domain. Let communities and governments pay for infrastructure. Lobby for tax breaks and tax credits. Privatize public resources and governmental services. The less visible the subsidies are, the better, but also support them with a constant repetition of the virtues of private enterprise, the rights of private property, and the equation of profits with happiness.

- *Externalize costs.* Underpay your employees, even if it means hiring children overseas to work twelve hours a day. Don't recycle your waste; don't clean it up if it's toxic; if you are caught, sue your insurance companies to make them pay. Minimize legal liability in general by claiming constitutional rights intended for natural persons.

- *Control information.* Acquire every outlet of the broadcast media, and merge their programs. Acquire independent publishers and bookstores, and standardize what they publish and sell. Write text books from a corporate point of view, and distribute them throughout the public school system. Pay the salaries of teachers and professors and social activists until they are no longer aware that they are censoring themselves for a living. Restrain free speech as much as possible. Forbid it on private property such as shopping malls. Forbid your employees to organize or to use the workplace as a venue for civic life. Make information about corporate operations and government decision making difficult to obtain. Worship expertise and confuse data with knowledge.

- *Centralize political authority.* Pay off injured employees and citizens to stay out of court, and make them agree to remain silent about the injury. If legal liability cannot be escaped, have it adjudicated in as high a court as possible. Do not appear in local or state courts if the case can be heard in federal court. Do not go to jury trial. If possible, preempt troublesome laws through the World Trade Organization, so that even national courts have less jurisdiction. Replace government and civic institutions with private corporations.

- *Centralize economic authority.* Acquire or destroy small businesses, cooperatives, and other alternatives. Make the surviving corporations as large as possible, not for economies of scale (which were optimized many decades ago), but for the sake of centralizing authority and eliminating competition. Have a handful of corporations dominate every industry, and have them control the allocation of resources and the means and the ends of production. Control prices. Remove profits from the community, and deposit them in offshore banks to escape taxes and potential liability.
- *Remove all barriers to trade,* regardless of whether they protect desirable industries, health and safety, human rights, or the environment. Expand management prerogative beyond the workplace, into the community, into the policymaking institutions, and across all jurisdictions. Make private property and the pursuit of profit the basis of all law and all social and economic policy. Create an economy where people have to pay currency for food, clothing, shelter, and culture. Commercialize the schools. Patent species. Make life pay.

Corporate power depends upon the successful maintenance of these principles. The cultural, legal, economic, and political mechanisms used to weave the web of power are complex, interdependent, and for most of us, largely hidden behind an invisible matrix of consensus reality. But the truth of the matter is that without subsidies, limited liability, and an inordinate influence over social and political agendas and information, corporations would soon become in reality what their apologists claim they are: merely groups of people. The sooner the better.

CULTURAL POWER:
THE COLONIZATION OF OUR MINDS

Economic and political power will not last long if is it is not rooted in the surrounding culture. Culture includes a society's usual ways of thinking, working, and living, as well as the largely unconscious beliefs and world views that make that way of life seem inevitable. Every society's beliefs, views, and customs become so embedded that its members come to believe that their own ways are not particular ways of acting, but simply follow natural and immutable laws.

The mass media, think tanks, public relations firms, and the education system deliver the corporate message into mainstream thinking. Lobbyists influence politicians. Think tanks and foundations influence teachers and students. Advertising influences consumers. The corporate construction of reality ridicules economic and political alternatives (public ownership, proportional representation) while promoting other views and choices (corporate financing of political campaigns, dependency on international trade) which come to seem inevitable.[5] As people cease to notice that some issues aren't discussed, their desires and beliefs are manipulated in an "engineering of consent," and eventually the entire society (including the powerless who would gain from political change) internalizes a truncated agenda which favors existing power relations.[6]

MASS MEDIA, MEDIA MONOPOLY

Journalists routinely expose corporate crime and corporate politics, but most people are simultaneously cynical and naïve about corruption so widespread it has become the norm. Even experienced activists often assume that the media serves a public interest function that other industries cannot be expected to serve. But the profits of the mass media depend on corporate advertising. The mass media's main product

---

Was there ever domination that did not appear natural to those who possess it?

19th century philospher and political economist John Stuart Mill

is no longer news, much less critical discourse. The purpose of the media is to deliver advertisements to target audiences.

As media ownership has become concentrated in fewer and fewer corporations, its own vested role in corporate power has increased. Through mergers, the media oligopoly is down to a handful of mega-corporations, including News Corporation, Viacom, Time Warner, Newhouse, General Electric, Westinghouse, Disney, Gannett, Knight-Ridder, Bertelsmann, and Elsevier. Media giant AOL Time Warner owns America Online, the biggest provider of e-mail and Internet service in the U.S. It also owns cable TV franchises with millions of viewers, the motion pictures which are broadcast on those cable stations, and book publishers and magazines. General Electric has long been known for electric power plants, nuclear energy, and weapons contracts. General Electric also owns NBC—as well as television and radio stations in New York, Los Angeles, Chicago, and many other cities.

The media industry now ranks (along with the energy industries, military contractors, airlines, and investment firms) among the leading lobbyists of the U.S. Congress. Between 1996 and 1998, media corporations and associations spent $111 million lobbying Congress; the top spenders included the National Association of Broadcasters, Time Warner, the National Cable Television Association, Walt Disney, and Viacom.[7] In return, Congress passed legislation quite profitable to the industry, ranging from the deregulation of ownership in multiple markets and media, to an array of tax breaks, to the giveaway of public broadcast spectrums.

More and more of the population is inundated with corporate advertising from fewer and fewer media outlets. Although U.S. law forbids non-commercial broadcasters from airing any kind of advertisements, the Public Broadcasting System (PBS) is also increasingly reliant on corporate commercials, which it calls "enhanced under-writer acknowledgments." PBS programs such as Sesame Street are funded by corporations such as the drug company Pfizer, Looksmart.com (a "family-oriented" Internet portal), the shopping website Toysmart.com, McDonald's, and Kellogg.[8]

The average person in the United States watches 37 hours of television a week, including an average of 714 commercials—that's 1,856 hours and 37,000 commercials per year. It is not only U.S. residents that are inundated with U.S. media; two thirds of Latin American

A good source for news and analysis of the media is the *Columbia Journalism Review*, which also tracks mergers and ownership at its website *www.cjr.org/owners/*

television programming actually originates in the United States.

Substantial news coverage has declined as advertising becomes the purpose of publishing and broadcasting. Media corporations want people to read newspapers and watch television programs in order to become consumers of the products being advertised. Advertising rates are based on the size of the audience. Sophisticated research allows ads to target specific populations ("narrowcasting") such as the elderly, or children under the age of five, or women, or college graduates. Get the consumer's attention, spark their interest by appealing to their subconscious self-images, create a desire, and lead them to the purchase—and collect personal information about them for more research and marketing. Nonconformists and dissidents are targeted with "liberation marketing" which portrays particular brands of computers, autos, soap, and soda pop as anti-establishment. Reluctant consumers are enticed with "green marketing" which implies that by buying certain products, they will liberate the earth.[9]

Two-thirds of the world's advertising takes place in the United States: in 1997, corporations spent $187 billion on television, radio, newspaper, magazine, billboard, telephone directory, direct mail, and Internet advertisements. Japan is the second-largest market, with twelve percent of the total advertising expense. The advertising industry, like others, has become concentrated in recent years, with the top firms, including WPP, Omnicom, Interpublic, Havas, Dentsu, and Saatchi & Saatchi, accounting for the lion's share of global ad revenues. As the lines between marketing, advertising, and public relations disappear, the top firms are gathering under the same corporate roofs.[10]

PUBLIC RELATIONS: SMOOTHING THE ROUGH EDGES

The public relations industry in the U.S. and worldwide has grown twenty to thirty percent annually in recent years.[11] Among the 500 largest U.S. corporations, the average budget for public relations and public affairs in 1998 was more than $4 million. If you count the money spent on department management, foundation support, social responsibility and corporate image advertising, the average budget for PR rose to about $25 million. Telecommunications, energy, and consumer products corporations were the highest spenders.[12]

Burson-Marsteller, one of the world's largest public relations firms, has 60 offices in 27 countries. Burson-Marsteller's clients have included A.H. Robbins (during the Dalkon shield IUD controversy), Tylenol (after its poison/tampering incidents), Union Carbide (after the toxic explosion in Bhopal India), Babcock & Wilcox (after the Three Mile Island nuclear accident), Exxon (after the Valdez Alaska oil spill),

Hydro-Quebec (on its James Bay projects), Mexico (as it lobbied for U.S. approval of the NAFTA trade agreement), and various military juntas and dictatorships such as Nigeria (during the Biafran war) and Romania (during the reign of Nicolae Ceausescu). Until 2000, Burson-Marsteller was owned by the advertising-PR-marketing giant Young & Rubicam, when Y&R was acquired by its rival WPP.[13]

EDUCATING THE PUBIC, INCORPORATING PUBLIC EDUCATION

Academia is fertile ground for planting ideas and legitimizing corporate goals, and the academies can lend a façade of institutional legitimacy and intellectual objectivity to what is actually business propaganda.[14] Corporate foundations give billions of dollars to think tanks, research institutes, and universities. Corporate executives are the largest single group represented on governing boards of colleges and universities.[15] Corporation-influenced think tanks have been established on university campuses across the country. A prominent example is the ultraconservative Hoover Institution on War, Revolution and Peace, which is housed and funded by Stanford University *(see profile of Hoover Institution in Part 2)*.[16]

Ultraconservative corporate foundations donate millions of dollars each year to influence political science, law, and economics departments at dozens of universities. The John M. Olin and Sarah Scaife Foundations give funding to Cornell, Harvard, Yale, Johns Hopkins, Loyola, Michigan State University, Princeton, Stanford, the U.S. Military and Naval Academies, the Universities of California, Illinois, Kansas, Maryland, and Virginia, Toronto, and Oxford. Professors who are willing to push the corporate agenda receive salaries and research contracts from corporations. Chairs and departments are often named after their benefactors.

- Bell South Professor of Education through Telecommunication at the University of South Carolina
- McLamore/Burger King Chair at the University of Miami
- John McCoy-BancOne Corp Professor of Creativity and Innovation at Stanford University
- John M. Olin Professor of Humanities at New York University
- Olin Professor of Law and Economics at Yale Law School
- Sears Roebuck Professor of Economics and Financial Services at the University of Chicago
- Ronald Reagan Professor of Public Policy at Pepperdine University
- James Baker III Institute for Public Policy at Rice University
- Center for the Study of American Business at Washington University
- Center for Corporate Community Relations at Boston College

Twelve thousand U.S. public schools (including forty percent of U.S. high schools) have contracts with Channel One, a corporate "news" and advertising network. Eight million students are required to watch Channel One at least one hour a week (or 31 hours a year—a full instruction week of school).[17] The Wall Street investment firm Kohlberg Kravis Roberts (which pioneered the leveraged corporate buyouts of the 1980s) owns 82 percent of PRIMEDIA, which owns Channel One. PRIMEDIA is a $1.7 billion publisher of consumer and trade magazines (*Seventeen, Modern Bride, American Baby*), and also distributes educational videos, provides satellite-delivered workplace training programs, produces trade shows, and owns and operates hundreds of Web sites and other Internet properties.[18]

Channel One is just one example of commercialism in public schools. Corporations fund sports events and other school activities; enjoy monopoly contracts to sell goods and services in exchange for sharing the profit with the schools; display their logos and advertisements on scoreboards, walls, and bulletin boards; write and distribute textbooks; and are buying schools and school programs which are then run for profit.[19]

FOUNDATIONS AND THINK TANKS:
EDUCATING THE PUBLIC, PERSUADING THE LAWMAKERS

Conservative, liberal, and libertarian philosophies can all serve the corporate agenda. For example, the conservative Heritage Foundation, the centrist Brookings Institution, and the libertarian Cato Institute are three of the major think tanks pushing corporate globalization. The top twenty conservative think tanks doubled their budgets between 1992 and 1997, and spent more than $1 billion in the 1990s. Five of the more influential organizations (Heritage, American Enterprise Institute, Brookings, Cato, and Institute for International Economics) had combined budgets of more than $77 million in 1995, compared to budgets totaling $19 million for eight liberal think tanks. Corporate think tanks are funded by ultra-conservative foundations such as John M. Olin, Scaife, Lilly, Carthage, and Coors. More socially-moderate but still pro-business foundations include Ford, Rockefeller, Pew, and Carnegie.[20] Other conservative foundations include:[21]

- Roe Foundation
- Charles G. Koch Foundation
- David H. Koch Foundation
- J. M. Foundation
- Castle Rock Foundation
- M. J. Murdock Charitable Trust

- Samuel Roberts Nobel Foundation
- John William Pope Foundation
- Earhart Foundation
- Richard and Helen DeVos Foundation
- Lynde and Harry Bradley Foundation
- Claude R. Lambe Charitable Foundation
- Lilly Endowment
- Gordon and Mary Cain Foundation
- Alec C. Walker Foundation
- Philip M. McKenna Foundation
- E.L. Wiegand Foundation
- Milliken Foundation

An article in the journal of the Council on Foreign Relations *(see profile of CFR in Part 2)* described the "new dynamics that are shaping public opinion in the United States. The new conservatism is dominating intellectual debate, because foundations committed to it understand that ideas and ideological commitment do count, and they are prepared to devote massive support to promote them." The article pointed out that "a tiny handful of think tanks and journals promoting the new conservatism received a major share" of the hundreds of millions spent by conservative think tanks, and that "it is this sort of concentration and coordination of financial efforts that makes the funding available to neoconservative thinkers so different from that awarded to scholars of alternative persuasions."[22]

Most think tanks are tax-exempt public education organizations forbidden by IRS regulations to spend a major portion of their resources on lobbying. But think tank "scholars" testify before Congressional committees, provide analyses and briefing papers to legislators, and periodically serve as government officials. As the CFR journal reported, "more and more think tanks hire public relations professionals, spend much of their time producing press releases rather than reports, and search for senior fellows who are media savvy or politically committed." The Heritage Foundation spends more on raising money and promoting its agenda than it does on funding research.[23]

LEGAL AND POLITICAL POWER: LEVERAGING AUTHORITY

Corporations dominate public policy making via lobbying, formal advisory committees, political campaign financing, and a constantly revolving door between business and government. Each of these mechanisms of influence is supposed to be regulated. U.S. laws require lobbying contracts and conflicts of interest to be disclosed. Other laws limit the amount of money individuals and corporations can donate to political campaigns. U.S. government officials are required to wait for a period of time before lobbying their former colleagues. But the laws that ostensibly limit political influence are ridden with loopholes, and are inadequate at best. Corporate power does more than influence the legal and political system—corporate power created the system we have today.

CORPORATE LAW

The monarchies of Europe gave corporate charters to multinational ventures. These chartered companies, in return for a percentage of the profit from their ventures, were given the authority to establish formal colonies, to write trade agreements and set up free trade zones, to seize competitors' ships, to maintain forts and armies, and to coin money. The companies levied taxes and ran the colonial courts, bribed local leaders with luxury goods and seats at the governors' table, and used slave labor to cut timber, dredge canals, and work the plantations. The colonial monopolies had enormous power, but legally their power was granted and withdrawn at the pleasure of the king.

Over the past 200 years, all over the world but especially in the United States, legal systems have been changed to accomplish two things: limit the legal liability of corporations, and give corporations

A political leader must keep looking over his shoulder all the time to see if the boys are still there. If they aren't there, he's no longer a political leader.

Bernard Baruch, 1965

the rights and protections of citizens. During the nineteenth century, U.S. state laws which required corporations to obtain a charter authorizing them to operate were replaced by general incorporation laws which simply require a form to be filled out and a registration fee to be paid. While this may seem more democratic (you no longer need to know the king to start a corporation), it also means that a legislature is not examining and defining each proposed incorporation.

By the end of the nineteenth century, the U.S. courts had declared that corporations were to be considered persons under the law—and then used this legal fiction of "personhood" to extend constitutional protections to corporations. The courts have ruled that corporate advertising and political campaign contributions are to be protected as free speech. Protection from unreasonable search and seizure has been used to thwart occupational health and safety inspections. The commerce clause of the constitution is interpreted by the courts to prohibit local and state governments from having regulations which might affect interstate commerce. Anti-monopoly laws have been interpreted to prohibit labor unions from going on strike, because a work stoppage would be a restraint on trade.

The legal liability of corporate executives has been limited, even in cases of negligence and fraud, and corporations seek "tort reform" which would limit the amount of money a corporation could be charged for injuring someone. The money spent to defend a corporation and its directors is tax-deductible. As a result of these laws and court rulings, corporations have more privileges and less liability than individuals. Negligence and fraud that would land an individual in jail are excused if the individual acted as a corporate executive. If corporate executives do happen to be held liable for some act, it is likely that the fine will be paid from the corporate treasury.

Beginning with the Interstate Commerce Commission in 1887, a maze of regulatory agencies has been constructed to limit the agendas and outcomes of every political struggle to deal with the impacts of corporate power, from monopoly to pollution to unemployment and poverty. In the process, government has become a shield between corporations and the people, and direct challenges to corporate power are channeled into endless administrative "remedies" which have exhausted generations of activists.[24]

Another result of the transformation of corporate law has been

---

Lobbyists are the touts of protected industries.

Winston Churchill

the destruction of the "free market" which corporate propagandists are constantly defending. A market is a self-correcting system which requires that the costs and benefits of economic activities are disclosed, that all parties are informed, are able to make rational choices, and will be held liable for their actions. None of these are the case. For example, food products contain toxic chemicals which are not disclosed, so people cannot choose whether to expose themselves. If someone does sue the manufacturer, it is unlikely that the true cost of the injury will be established, or that the corporation will be held liable. The corporate-dominated economic and legal system cannot provide the feedback and self-correction that would characterize a true market system.

FORMAL AND INFORMAL ADVISORY GROUPS

The relationship most corporations and industry associations have with government is informal, in that their advice is unofficial, but governments also appoint formal advisory committees. Despite laws requiring them to represent a balance of society's views and interests, these committees are dominated by corporations and industry associations, and serve as a "major institutional method for linking private interests and private expertise to public authorities."[25]

Eighty percent of the U.S. Presidential advisory commissions appointed between World War II and the early 1970s to deal with some aspect of foreign or military policy were headed by members of the Council on Foreign Relations, and two of the other commissions were headed by trustees of the Committee for Economic Development (CED).[26] Of five commissions offering advice on government reorganization and salaries, four were headed by CED trustees.[27]

Industry Sector Advisory Committees, created by the Trade Act of 1974, formally advise the U.S. Trade Representative on matters relating to U.S. trade policy. Members of the ISACs are appointed by the U.S. Secretary of Commerce and the U.S. Trade Representative, and represent corporations and associations in aerospace, chemicals, electronics, lumber, construction, and other industries.

Similar bodies advise European policymakers in national govern-

---

Why is it legitimate to invite a member of Congress to make a speech before a trade association and pay him $5,000 when everyone knows he has nothing to say? Isn't that a subtle form of corruption?

Peter Nehemkis of the UCLA School of Management, in Money Talks

ments, the European Union, and the European Parliament *(see the profiles of the European Roundtable of Industrialists and the Union of Industrial and Employers' Confederations of Europe in Part 2).*

REVOLVING DOORS AND INTERLOCKS: THE KEYS TO THE CLUB

Members of advisory commissions are often former (or future) government officials. Former corporate executives commonly head regulatory agencies. When bureaucrats quit government service they are often hired by corporations, so many retired members and staff of Congress and government agencies lobby their former colleagues on behalf of their new employers. Corporate executives are not just lobbyists and bureaucrats — they serve as the heads of cabinets and ministries.

U.S. President John F. Kennedy appointed Dean Rusk, the president of the Rockefeller Foundation, to be his Secretary of State. Ford Motor president Robert McNamara, who later served as the head of the World Bank, was Kennedy's Secretary of Defense. Investment banker C. Douglas Dillon was Kennedy's Secretary of the Treasury.

Ronald Reagan uniformly appointed "the consummate old boys of the country's political-corporate network."[28] Before becoming U.S. President, Reagan himself had promoted nuclear power as a paid spokesman for General Electric. Reagan's cabinet was dominated by officers and directors of multinational corporations such as Bechtel and Pepsico, as well as from pro-corporate policy groups such as the Trilateral Commission, the Business Roundtable, and the Council on Foreign Relations.[29]

At least 23 of President Bill Clinton's appointees were members of the Council on Foreign Relations, and nine of them, including his Secretaries of State, Defense, and Human and Health Services, were CFR directors. The revolving door has connected the Clinton Cabinet with major manufacturers (Lockheed Martin, Union Carbide, and Ford Motors), banks and investment firms (Goldman Sachs and Citigroup), corporate foundations and think tanks (Rockefeller, Carnegie, and Brookings Institution), and public relations firms (Hill & Knowlton and Timmons).[30]

Good sources of information on political campaign finance include Common Cause, the Center for Responsive Politics, and the Center for Public Integrity. These organizations provide valuable analysis and summaries, and maintain up-to-date websites which make U.S. Federal Election Commission data available. *www.commoncause.org, www.crp.org* or *www.opensecrets.org, www.publicintegrity.org.*

The dominance of the U.S. government by men with elite backgrounds is not new. According to a detailed study of Cabinet officers, diplomats, and Supreme Court Justices during the two hundred years from 1780 to 1980, the overwhelming majority came from the highest ranks of personal wealth. More than three-fourths of the 205 Cabinet secretaries appointed between 1897 and 1972 were directors of corporations or came from corporate law firms — with no significant difference between Republican and Democratic appointees.[31]

LOBBYING AND POLITICAL INFLUENCE-BUYING

Still not content with being formal advisors and cabinet secretaries, corporations and their associations, lobbyists, and consultants have instituted political campaign finance arrangements — the current euphemism for buying politicians. In 1970, only 175 corporations in the U.S. had registered lobbyists, and only a handful of corporations had public affairs departments. Ten years later, 650 corporations had registered lobbyists, more than 80 percent of the Fortune 500 had formal public affairs offices, and corporate representatives in Washington outnumbered federal employees. By 1980:

- 12,000 lawyers represented corporations before federal regulatory agencies and federal courts
- 9,000 business lobbyists and 50,000 trade-association staff promoted favorable legislation
- 8,000 public relations and 1,300 public-affairs specialists promoted a favorable image for their corporate clients
- 12,000 specialized journalists reported on government actions affecting particular industries.[32]

The expansion in public relations has continued and has grown twenty to thirty percent annually in recent years.[33] There are now 14,000 registered lobbyists in Washington D.C., and 150,000 public relations professionals throughout the country. In 1997, corporations spent $1.26 billion on lobbying Congress — $2.4 million for each member of Congress.[34]

Financial services/insurance/real estate was the top industry for lobbying in 1998 (spending $203 million), followed by communications/

A criminal is a person with predatory instincts
who has not sufficient capital to form a corporation.

Howard Scott, founder of
The Technical Alliance and Technocracy, Inc.

electronics, health, energy/natural resources, agriculture, and transportation ($116 million). The military industry spent almost $48 million in 1998 *(see chart below)*.[35] The top five U.S. lobbying firms in 1998 were Cassidy & Associates ($20 million receipts), Verner Liipfert, Patton Boggs, Akin Gump, and Preston Gates ($10 million receipts). Their clients that year ranged from Boeing to Boston University to Philip Morris to the Puerto Rico Economic Development Administration *(see Appendices 1 and 2 for lists of the top lobbyists and spenders)*.[36]

Most of the money spent on election campaigns in the United States comes from corporations. Several organizations track the campaign contributions that are required to be disclosed to the public, but most of the money given to political candidates is not disclosed. As pointed out by William Greider in his book *Who Will Tell the People*, even if it were, there is a more fundamental disorder to the political system that goes well beyond simple bribery. The entire political system is based on money-based bargaining, in which politicians see corporations as constituents and industries as clients. Periodic scandals of illegal campaign contributions simply distract the public from the

Industries Ranked by Spending on Lobbying and Political Campaigns [37]

Industry	1998 Lobbying Expenditures	1997-98 Polical Campaign Contributions
Finance, Insurance and Real Estate	$ 202,753,235	$ 154,414,056
Communications/Electronics	186,491,891	54,553,753
Health [sic] (insurance, drugs, doctors, etc.)	165,419,816	58,803,092
Energy and Natural Resources	143,811,418	41,146,858
Agriculture	119,332,772	43,262,232
Transportation	115,637,143	35,531,510
Defense	48,708,502	11,431,320
Construction	22,342,322	32,857,600
Miscellaneous Business	172,476,218	90,553,748
Total registered spending by corporations	1,176,975,243	522,556,068
Total by labor unions	24,000,000	61,000,000

It should be noted that the table above shows political influence-buying in an off year. Campaign contributions during the 1999-2000 Presidential election cycle hit $2 billion even before the final, most expensive month of the campaign.

more fundamental reality of "hundreds of millions of dollars invested by powerful economic interests every year in the Washington decision-making process."[38] Sociologist G. William Domhoff has written that "lobbyists from corporations, law firms, and trade associations play a key role in shaping government on key issues of concern to specific corporations or business sectors, but their importance should not be overestimated because a majority of those elected to Congress are pre-disposed to agree with them."[39]

Money has become so crucial to being elected to political office in the United States that one can without much hyperbole say that politicians are elected by dollars, not votes, and that their constituents are now corporations rather than people. Indeed, since 1976, the two U.S. Presidential candidates who raised the most money by the end of the year preceding the election have become the Democratic and Republican candidates. In effect, it is corporations and industry associations which determine the candidates who will run for office — and many corporations give to both parties, ensuring access no matter which candidate wins.

The money can be substantial. In the 1998 Senate elections, races in ten states spent more than $7 million; two races in California and Illinois spent more than $20 million, and the New York race between Alfonse D'Amato and Charles Schumer totaled almost $36 million. The 2000 Senate races in New York and New Jersey cost more than $48 million.[40]

Where does the money go? Much of it goes to the media corporations that own the television networks which run the advertisements to elect the candidates the corporations want. Media income from political campaign advertisement reached $600 million in 2000.

U.S. law prohibits corporations and labor unions from making contributions or expenditures to influence federal elections. The law also limits the amount an individual can give to a political candidate to $1,000 per election. So how can millions of dollars be given to political campaigns? Corporations, unions and other organizations,

---

I get a little bit distressed because the fact is that it's so well-known there is so much money required to run for reelection that the general public gets the impression . . . that members of Congress never cast a vote until they go back and read the list of who contributed to their campaign or took them out to dinner or something. And that is absolutely nonsensical.

U.S. House Minority Leader Robert Michel, quoted in Speaking Freely, *Center for Responsive Politics.*

and individuals are allowed to give their money to Political Action Committees (PACs). PACs were first used by labor unions to pool the contributions of their members as a way to offset the monetary clout of big business. In 1974, during the Watergate "reforms," Congress eliminated a regulation which forbade companies and unions that got government contracts from forming PACs. Another floodgate was opened when the Federal Election Commission ruled that corporate PACs could pool contributions from both shareholders and employees.[41] The current rules allow each PAC to give up to $5,000 to a candidate per election, and donate up to $15,000 to a national party committee per year — *but a corporation may form any number of PACs.*

An even larger loophole in the limits on money in politics is "soft money." Soft money was invented by a 1979 Federal Election Commission ruling which allowed direct corporate contributions and unlimited individual contributions to political parties as long as the money is not used to support a particular candidate by name. Soft money is often spent on "issue ads" which praise or criticize candidates, but do not use the words "vote for" or "vote against." Soft money contributions, which were not required to be disclosed until 1991, totaled $89 million in the 1992 election cycle, $263 million in 1996, and stood at a record $256 million for the first 18 months of the 1999-2000 election cycle.[42] Many corporations (AT&T, Phillip Morris, Microsoft, and Citigroup among the largest) give hundreds of thousands of dollars to both parties, ensuring access no matter which party wins a given seat in the next elections *(see Appendix 3 for list of the top soft money contributors).*[43]

"Bundled money" is another innovation to get around the legal limits on how much an individual or corporation may donate to a political candidate, in which a lobbyist or PAC gathers separate donations from a number of individuals and then "bundles" them together before delivery to the candidate.[44]

Local governments have entered the lobbying contest, just to keep up with the corporations. A lobbyist for an association of counties in Wisconsin said he "used to focus on gathering information and persuading legislators with the facts . . . but that doesn't seem to be

---

All parties, however loyal to principals at first, degenerate into aristocracies of interest at last; and unless a nation is capable of discerning the point where integrity ends and fraud begins, popular parties are among the surest modes of introducing an aristocracy.

John Taylor, 1814

enough anymore, with so many groups spending so much money on campaigns. It puts individual legislators in an awfully tough spot to side with us against those who have spent a lot of money on their campaigns. . . . My members are very frustrated by what appears to be the growing dominance of big money in the campaign process." The League of Wisconsin Municipalities is considering creating its own Political Action Committee, and in the meantime has urged city officials to make personal campaign contributions. (Cities are prohibited from making campaign contributions, but city officials are not). The counties also considered forming a PAC, but had decided that "it wasn't right for one level of government to have to pay to gain access to another level of government."[45]

ECONOMIC POWER: AVENUES OF WEALTH

What are generally called subsidies (and have now been dubbed "corporate welfare") are various forms of privatization or externalization—the fundamental processes by which corporations build and maintain power and wealth. There are dozens of methods by which corporations privatize the benefits and externalize the costs onto communities, workers, taxpayers, and nature. Limited liability, corporate personhood, political financing, and corporate tax breaks are the legal and economic mechanisms by which privatization and externalization are implemented.

- When governments impose wage controls, forbid union organizing, or end labor strikes, the resulting cheap labor is a subsidy to corporate employers.
- Public resources such as electricity, and natural resources such as water and timber, are sold to corporations below cost and at unsustainable rates.[46]
- Much of the U.S. federal budget is essentially welfare for a few corporate manufacturers of weapons, missiles, and airplanes *(see section on the military on page 42).*
- Government agencies regularly bail out corporations which are threatened with bankruptcy, and subsidize entire industries when economic conditions threaten profits.
- National and local governments offer tax breaks and grants to corporations to provide jobs, attract investment, and benefit political allies.
- Publicly-funded export credit agencies provide loans, insurance, and marketing services to corporations which operate overseas *(see discussion on export credit on page 32).*
- Commercial bank loans to Southern nations were unloaded onto

---

Government does not solve problems—it subsidizes them.

Ronald Reagan, December 11, 1972

the World Bank and IMF in the 1980s — in effect, externalized onto the public *(see section on banks on page 29)*.

- The World Bank and International Monetary Fund are forcing the sale of public property and public resources around the world to corporations *(see the profile of the World Bank in Part 2)*.

Recent studies estimate that direct tax breaks and grants to corporations in the U.S. are worth more than $100 billion every year *(see Appendix 5 for list of studies)*. Such studies are helpful in revealing some of the worst abuses of corporate subsidies — but they reveal only the tip of the iceberg, because they measure only direct subsidies. A more meaningful measure of the costs of doing business is externalities, that is, any transfer of the costs of doing business from the corporation to some other sector of society or to the environment. Externalities range from the health care costs of automobile pollution and dangerous consumer products, to the cost of cleaning up toxic waste abandoned by manufacturers, to fraudulent cost overruns by doctors, health insurance companies, and weapons manufacturers.

Measuring externalities provides a more complete measure of the subsidies provided to corporations. Externalities are more difficult to calculate than direct tax breaks and payments, but they are not impossible to estimate. Corporate accountant Ralph Estes has credibly documented externalities of $2.5 trillion per year — 25 times greater than most estimates of direct budget subsidies.[47] As David Korten pointed out in *The Post-Corporate World*, since total U.S. corporate profits are about $500 billion per year, the externalized costs outweigh profits by five to one[48] — not a very efficient system, even from the narrowest consideration of providing goods and services efficiently.

The modern corporation is a legal structure that limits liability and privatizes profit. Privatization and externalization are the foundation, and the Achilles heel, of the industrial system and of the corporate form of doing business. Proposals to trim a few tax breaks may actually serve to perpetuate a system that is dependent on the misallocation of benefits and costs.

Nothing is illegal if a hundred businessmen decide to do it, and that's true anywhere in the world.

Andrew Young,
The Speakers Electronic Reference Collection, *1994*

We are in the midst of the greatest wave of corporate mergers in history. The first wave of mega-mergers occurred at the turn of the twentieth century, when industries such as steel, petroleum, and rubber were consolidated under a few giant corporations. These mergers may actually have been promoted by the Sherman Act of 1890, which forbade collusion in the form of price-fixing and market division, but did not outlaw mergers themselves. The consolidation of industry was continued in a second wave in the 1910s and 1920s. During a third wave of mergers in the 1950s and 1960s, many small and medium-sized corporations in different industries were gathered up by conglomerates such as Textron and ITT. In the 1980s, corporate mergers and acquisitions were characterized by hostile takeovers and leveraged buyouts. Since the 1980s, deregulation of one industry after another (airlines in 1978, trucking and railroads in 1980, natural gas in 1981 and 1985, banking in 1980 and 1982 and 1999, telecommunications in 1977 and 1984 and 1996) has promoted another wave of mega-mergers. The overwhelming majority of the largest corporate mergers in history have occurred in the last few years.[49]

When an industry is controlled by a handful of corporations, it is called an oligopoly — "a few sellers." When ostensible competitors conspire to fix prices, to allocate customers by dividing markets, or to pool their receipts in a way that reduces competition, it is called collusion. If a number of those restraints on free trade are agreed to by an oligopoly, the result is a cartel. Classic cartels have been built in electrical manufacturing, oil and gas, petrochemicals, steel, and other industries.

At the turn of the twentieth century, John D. Rockefeller gained control of the emerging U.S. oil industry through secret deals with the railroads that hauled his oil, through buying up refineries, oil fields, and pipelines, by controlling prices and dividing markets, and by forcing his rivals out of business.

The various Rockefeller corporations were controlled by a holding company called Standard Oil of New Jersey. In 1911, the U.S. courts declared Standard Oil to be an illegal monopoly, and ordered that it should be broken up into separate corporations — but this did not last. The mid-century petroleum oligopoly, dubbed the Seven Sisters, consisted

---

The business of government is to keep government out of business —
that is, unless business needs government aid.

Will Rogers

of the "separate" Standard Oil corporations from New Jersey, New York, and California, plus Texaco, Gulf, Shell, and British Petroleum. But by the end of the century, Standard Oil of California (aka Socal and Chevron) had acquired Gulf. Standard Oil of Indiana merged with Amoco. Standard Oil of Ohio (and Amoco) have merged with British Petroleum. Standard Oil of New York (aka Socony or Mobil) has now merged with Standard Oil of New Jersey (aka Exxon). These corporations are further combined into joint ventures around the world.[50]

Periodic anti-monopoly action by government sheds light on the continuing concentration of industry, but does little else, and there has been a steady demise in enforcement over the twentieth century. Most industries are now controlled by a few major corporations *(see Appendix 4 for list of the 500 largest corporations).*[51]

As the U.S. Congress was writing laws to regulate the monopolies, the courts were interpreting the Constitution's commerce clause to strike down hundreds of local and state government laws that had been passed to regulate corporations. This turned the infant anti-trust law on its head, and allowed *corporations* to sue *local governments* for restraining their economic activities. Recent trade treaties have extended such rulings to the international level, and corporations now sue *national* governments for restraining *international* trade. Any "barrier" to trade is liable to be attacked, whether it is designed to protect a local industry, the public's health, or the environment.[52] From the corporate point of view, this is just the logical extension of U.S. court rulings striking down local and state regulation—always tending toward centralized power.

Entire national economies can be affected by the actions and fortune of a single corporation. Even as it laid off 99,000 U.S. workers between 1992 and 1996, General Motors became the largest private employer in Mexico by moving its operations south of the border. Union workers are being replaced by lower-paid contract and temporary workers, and Manpower, a temporary employment agency, is now the largest employer in the United States.[53]

Corporations squeeze higher profits from fewer and lower-paid workers, many of whom no longer receive pensions, health insurance, or other benefits. Corporate executives are taking fatter salaries and

---

There is not one grain of anything in the world that is sold in the free market. Not one. The only place you see a free market is in the speeches of politicians.

Wayne Andreas, chairman of Archer Daniels Midland, quoted in Z Magazine, *April 1997*

stock options, and reinvesting less in corporate operations. The fastest way to boost corporate stock prices is to announce a merger between two corporations, followed by the layoff of thousands of workers to "streamline operations."[54]

POLITICAL RISK INSURANCE

Globalization takes corporations into dangerous territory. Indigenous peoples and traditional farmers may resent the industrial development of their traditional lands. Foreign countries may revise their tax structures in ways that reduce a corporation's profit margin. Revolutions may threaten the nationalization of mining and manufacturing operations dating back to colonial times. When private insurers and investors are unwilling to accept the risks, corporations turn to national and multilateral government agencies which offer investment guarantees and political risk insurance backed by taxpayers.

National agencies which sell risk insurance include the U.S. Overseas Private Investment Corporation, Japan's Overseas Economic Cooperation Fund, and Canada's Export Development Corporation. Multilateral agencies include World Bank affiliates such as the Multilateral Investment Guarantee Agency (MIGA) and International Finance Corporation (IFC), and regional banks such as the Inter-American Development Bank (IADB).

These public agencies provide billions of dollars worth of insurance to thousands of corporations in order to guarantee their profits. There are various types of insurance.[55]

- *Inconvertibility of currency,* which protects investors from increased restrictions on the investor's ability to "convert local currency into U.S. dollars" (in other words, remove their profits from the host country).
- *Expropriation insurance* provides compensation for losses due to host government actions which "deprive the investor of its fundamental rights in the investment." This includes confiscation, expropriation, nationalization, "creeping nationalization" by

The growth of a large business is merely a survival of the fittest, the working out of law of nature and a law of God ... The time was ripe for it. It had to come, though all we saw at the moment was the need to save ourselves from wasteful conditions ... The day of combination is here to stay. Individualism has gone, never to return.

John D. Rockefeller, quoted in Alan Trachtenberg,
The Incorporation of America, *1982*

government participation in corporate enterprises, or through restricting the transfer of shares or profits. Even balance of payment problems, national planning priorities, protection of local industry, restrictions on currency conversion, or unattractive exchange rates or tax laws can be considered "expropriation."

- *Political risk insurance* covers investors against losses caused not only by "politically motivated acts of violence" such as war, coup d'etat, revolution, insurrection or civil strife, terrorism, sabotage, strikes, distribution problems, or "bureaucratic delays."

The U.S. government's investment guarantee program began in 1948, and corporate executives in other countries soon felt that the subsidized insurance put them at a disadvantage, and urged their governments to institute low-cost insurance as well. Japan began offering risk insurance in the 1950s, and West Germany in the 1960s, and by the early 1980s, sixteen of the industrialized countries had investment guarantee programs.[56]

Government insurance programs support their countries' economic and political policies. For example, Japan's Overseas Economic Cooperation Fund, which has made acquisition of raw materials a major objective, provides loans and political risk insurance for natural resource exploration in underdeveloped countries—and bases the cost of loan repayments and insurance premiums upon the cash flow of the project.[57]

In the early 1970s, the main political risk insurance agency in the United States, the Overseas Private Insurance Corporation (actually a subsidiary of the U.S. State Department), managed to get private insurance companies to reinsure its investment guarantee program, but private insurers refused to reinsure OPIC's war and insurrection liabilities. It took many years for private insurers to begin offering any form of political risk insurance, and they still offer less coverage at a higher price.[58] Attempts to privatize government insurance agencies have been unsuccessful for obvious reasons—government agencies are backed financially and politically by the endless resources of the public *(see profile of the U.S. Overseas Private Investment Corporation in Part 2).*

If monopoly persists, monopoly will always sit at the helm of government. I do not expect monopoly to restrain itself. If there are men in this country big enough to own the government of the United States, they are going to own it.

U.S. President Woodrow Wilson

Commercial banks and investment firms make money by buying shares of the stocks and bonds sold by corporations and governments. They also make money by selling and underwriting the sale of those stocks and bonds, and by arranging corporate mergers and acquisitions.

Most stocks and bonds are now owned by other corporations, not by people. These "institutional shareholders" may be corporations like Ford or Chase Manhattan Bank, or they may be pension funds such as the California Public Employees Retirement System.[59] Insurance companies, with billions in assets from the premiums paid by customers, are also major shareholders of corporate stock. Investment firms may also serve as "beneficial shareholders" by holding stocks and bonds for some other private or corporate entity. (Beneficial shareholding is done as a service to manage the portfolios of wealthy investors, but it also serves to shield the identity of the true shareholder).

Corporate and governmental financial institutions are intertwined in numerous ways. There are commercial banks and central banks. Central banks accept deposits from and make loans to commercial banks; they also set interest rates and exchange currencies with the central banks of other nations. While they are ostensibly an instrument of government control over national financial systems, central banks are typically private entities whose members are corporate banks. There are investment firms, which gamble billions of public and private dollars in complex financial instruments like commodities, futures, and hedge funds. There are national and multilateral agencies, which finance corporate investment with tax monies, provide export credit and insurance, and bail out some of the speculators when they fail. Free trade agreements between national governments have codified investment and trade rules, which further concentrate power and wealth.

Commercial and investment banks exercise power by deciding which corporations and which projects will be financed, and lending money often leads to direct ownership and control. In the early 1900s, the various partners of J.P. Morgan held 72 directorships in 47 corporations. By the late 1960s, Morgan Guaranty had interlocking directorships with 233 corporations, and held five percent or more of the shares of 270 corporations. Two firms, Morgan Guaranty and Chase

When I give food to the poor they call me a saint.
When I ask why the poor have no food, they call me a communist.

Brazilian Catholic Archbishop Don Helder Camara

Manhattan Bank, held five percent or more of the total stock of seven leading airlines. The directors of 49 U.S. banks also sat on the boards of 300 of the 500 largest U.S. corporations, and controlled 5 percent or more of the stock in 5,270 corporations—and acted as sole trustee for three-fourths of other people's money that they managed.[60]

In the past twenty years, the banking industry has been freed of regulations put in place during economic crises such as the Depression of the 1930s. For example, the savings and loan (S&L) banks in the United States were largely restricted to loaning money to homeowners, and the U.S. government insured the money that people deposited in S&L accounts. In the early 1980s, the S&Ls were deregulated, and they began to take in billions of dollars from investors who wanted higher rates of profit. The S&Ls began to invest their new "hot money" in speculative ventures such as office buildings and the corporate mergers of the 1980s. S&L executives also siphoned off much of the money and squandered it. By the end of the decade, half of the S&L banks were insolvent. Since the S&L deposits were insured by the U.S. government, they had to be paid back with tax money. Despite (or perhaps because of) evidence that executives at three-quarters of the insolvent S&Ls had engaged in fraud, the U.S. government delayed dealing with the problem for several years, and then chose to pay for the bailout with interest-bearing bonds over forty years. The wealthy who can afford to buy those bonds will make another round of profit, but it will triple the cost to U.S. taxpayers to $300 to $500 billion.

In 1999, U.S. commercial banking was also deregulated. Banks, stockbrokers, and insurance companies are now allowed to merge, and the Community Reinvestment Act, which required banks to loan a small percentage of bank deposits to low-income neighborhoods, was weakened.

Central banks have been defined as "the bankers' bank," as "the lender of last resort," and as "the instrument of government control of money and credit." Central banks accept deposits from commercial banks, they lend money back to those banks as well as to governments, they print money, they set interest rates, and they transfer money and gold to and from other countries. The policies set by the central banks have a huge impact on economic growth, employment,

---

All in all, I think we've hit the jackpot.

U.S. President Ronald Reagan, October 15, 1992, as he signed a bill
deregulating the savings and loan industry and allowing bankers
to squander and gamble hundreds of billions in U.S. taxpayers' money.

wages, and income distribution. While they are often portrayed as official government agencies, the central banks are usually private corporations made up of and controlled by corporate banks. Most industrialized countries have central banks. In the U.S., the central bank is the Federal Reserve System *(see the profile of the U.S. Federal Reserve Bank in Part 2)*.

The Bretton Woods agreements of 1944 included a fixed rate of exchange for the world's currencies, which were tied to the value of the U.S. dollar, which was backed by the U.S. government's promise to convert it to gold upon demand. In 1971, the U.S. abolished the gold standard, and since then the world's currencies have been allowed to "float" at whatever rates the "market" (dominated by financial speculators) determines. As Chalmers Johnson has written, the end of the Bretton Woods system "returned [the West] to the monetary barbarism and instability of the nineteenth century. Floating exchange rates introduced a major element of instability into the international trading system. They stimulated the growth of so-called finance capitalism—which refers to making money from trading stocks, bonds, currencies, and other forms of securities as well as lending money to companies, governments, and consumers rather than manufacturing products and selling them at prices determined by unfettered markets. Finance capitalism, as its name implies, means making money by manipulating money.[61]

Financial speculation has overtaken manufacturing and labor as the primary engine of the globalized economy. Unlike manufacturers, banks and investors prefer high interest rates and low inflation, and don't mind unemployment. In the past generation, the gap between rich and poor has increased, wages have fallen, unemployment and poverty have increased, and governments have lost the political will

---

The unrestricted flow of speculative capital in accordance with Washington Consensus doctrine was what our governments in East Asia institutionalized in the early 1990s, under the strong urging of the International Monetary Fund and the U.S. Treasury Department. The result: the $100 billion that flowed in between 1993 and 1997 flowed out in the bat of an eyelash during the Great Panic of the summer of 1997, bringing about the collapse of our economies and spinning them into a mire of recession and massive unemployment from which most still have to recover. Since 1997, financial instability of the constant erosion of our currencies has become a way of life under IMF-imposed monetary regimes that leave the value of our money to be determined day-to-day by the changing whims, moods, and preferences of foreign investors and currency speculators.

Walden Bello, "From Melbourne to Prague," September 2000

and the ability to direct development policy through social spending.[62] Public spending for development has decreased, while corporate investment in developing countries has soared. The Bank for International Settlements (BIS) in Basel, Switzerland was set up in the 1930s to be the central bank of the central banks; some of its functions have been taken over by the IMF *(see profile in Part 2)*, but the Basel Committee on Banking Supervision, which consists of senior representatives of the world's leading central banks, is currently trying to deal with the impacts and dangers of a global economy where productive investment is overwhelmed by financial speculation. This "casino economy" has exacerbated economic crises around the world and resulted in bail-outs of investment funds so large that their failure could set off regional and even global financial panics.

Export credit agencies (ECAs) are public agencies providing taxpayer-backed loans, loan guarantees,[63] and political risk insurance to corporations doing business overseas. Most industrialized countries now have at least one ECA, and together the world's ECAs now provide more financial backing than the World Bank.[64]

Much of the recent ECA loans and guarantees, at least $50 billion annually (more than all multilateral and bilateral aid agencies combined), has gone for large infrastructure projects such as dams, power plants, mining projects, oil pipelines, chemical and industrial facilities, and forestry plantations. "There is a stark contrast between the policies of the ECAs—which are oriented almost exclusively towards export promotion—and those of development assistance agencies (aid agencies) and multilateral development banks (like the World Bank Group).... The same [Organization for Economic Cooperation and Development] countries that have approved environmental and social policies for their aid agencies and the World Bank Group subvert them through their ECAs, which increasingly are financing projects and investments that bilateral and multilateral agencies reject on environmental, social, and economic grounds."[65]

Export credit agencies are the largest official creditors of developing countries. When debtor nations can no longer keep up the payments on these export credit loans, the World Bank and International Monetary Fund step in to restructure the debtor country's economy, which imposes corporate control and further exacerbates debt *(see section on page 33 on structural adjustment).*[66]

Multilateral and bilateral development banks were created for a number of ostensible reasons. The World Bank and International Monetary Fund were created to help countries recover from World War II and to stabilize the world's finances *(see profile of the World*

Bank and International Monetary Fund in Part 2). Regional institutions like the Asian, African, and Latin American Development Banks were created to foster economic growth and cooperation. The national governments of the richer nations provide "bilateral development assistance" to developing countries through their own agencies.

The impact of "development financing" is often to increase debt rather than to facilitate development and to enrich multinational corporations rather than to build domestic industries. Since the mid-1980s, the net flow of money has been from the South to the North, even though Southern debt has increased thirty-fold since 1970. Development bank approval of specific projects (such as hydroelectric dams, transportation infrastructure, and industrial facilities) jump-starts projects that encourage (and subsidize) commercial banks to go where they might not otherwise go. The development banks are so interlocked with agencies providing export credit and political risk insurance, and to the corporate financial system, that it is impossible to tell them apart. Governments providing "foreign aid" often require that the money be spent buying goods and services from corporations headquartered in the donor's country. Nearly half of all World Bank financing goes directly to the multinational corporations that are the real beneficiaries of "foreign aid" and "development assistance." The most destructive and notorious aspect of these programs has been the imposition of structural adjustment upon the debtor countries.

TRADE TREATIES AND STRUCTURAL ADJUSTMENT: FORCED PARTICIPATION IN THE CORPORATE ECONOMY

In 1970, the poorest nations owed about $21 billion to Northern banks and investors. Ten years later, their debt was $110 billion, and by the early 1980s, with defaults looming on some loans, commercial banks and investors were transferring the debt to national governments and public agencies such as the World Bank. The World Bank and the International Monetary Fund began to tie loans to "structural adjustment" programs, which channeled more of the debtor country's financial and productive resources toward debt repayment.

Structural adjustment involves "economic stabilization" and "structural reforms." These typically involve some form of the following:[67]

- The debtor nation is required to "liberalize" (increase) prices on basic goods such as food, consumer durables, tools and equipment, and energy. Overnight price increases of several hundred percent mean local businesses can no longer afford to ship their goods to market, and they are undercut by imported goods from subsidized agribusiness and other corporations from the North.

- Public employees are laid off, and government services are reduced. The most profitable state enterprises are "privatized" (sold to foreign corporations or investors). If public services are enshrined in the constitution (Brazil, Mexico), then the constitution is amended accordingly. Schools and health clinics are closed in order to redirect public monies toward "debt repayment" (Northern banks). Public works such as roads, hospitals, and water projects are redirected to international construction and engineering firms. Almost half of all World Bank financing goes directly to corporations, and some countries (including the UK) receive more funds from the Bank than they contribute.
- The "labor market is liberalized" to reduce public spending and to attract foreign corporations. Wages are "indexed" (cut), cost of living adjustments are eliminated, and minimum wage legislation is phased out.
- The IMF ensures the country's central bank is made "independent from political power" by taking it over. Officials of the central bank are replaced, often with former staff members of the multinational development banks. The government is prohibited from creating money or providing credit, which makes the country increasingly dependent on "outside sources" (Northern banks and investors) for funding, which further increases debt. During the 1980s, eighty percent of the commercial bank loans to the South never left the Northern banks.
- The country's banking system is "deregulated." Low-interest loans to farmers and local businesses are phased out. Interest rates are raised, attracting "hot money" from foreign investors looking for quick profits. State banks are privatized, with the proceeds directed towards external debt service. Under a 1994 GATT agreement, foreign banks are allowed free entry into domestic banking.
- Capital movement is "liberated," allowing foreign investors to move "hot" money in and out of the country with no regard for long-term productive investment. Foreign exchange (the ability to turn the domestic currency into dollars or other foreign currencies) is also "freed," allowing foreign corporations to repatriate (remove) profits. Southern elites who have stolen public funds, "dirty money" profits from illegal activities, and "black money" which has escaped taxation is also removed from the country—and usually deposited in Northern banks or offshore banking havens.
- Trade is "liberalized." Tariffs are eliminated, which reduces customs revenues (money from taxes on imported goods). Import quotas which protected local industries are eliminated,

which opens the domestic economy to cheap imports from multinational corporations.

- "Tax reform" such as sales taxes are instituted, which disproportionately impact the poor. Taxes are instituted on small agricultural producers and informal urban industries, while foreign investments and joint ventures receive "tax holidays" in order to attract "foreign direct investment" (Northern corporations).
- Customary land rights are abolished. Land is parceled and sold (with the proceeds going to external debt payments). Land is soon concentrated into private hands, and farmers who formerly used the commons become landless seasonal workers for agribusinesses which grow food for export.

Structural adjustments were originally imposed on an ad hoc basis upon individual nations when it appeared that they could not keep up with existing debt payments. By 1985, fifteen debtor nations had been subjected to SAPs, and by 1991, a quarter of the World Bank's total lending was tied to structural adjustment in 54 nations. As more of the "debtor" nations' dwindling resources went to debt service, new loans were simply used to repay previous loans, and the total debt of the low income nations more than quadrupled from $100 to $473 billion between 1980 and 1992.

World Bank and IMF "reforms" continued, and by the mid-1990s, more than a hundred countries and 80 percent of the world's population had been "structurally adjusted." The average developing nation's debt payments were a third of its gross national product; Peru's payments totaled half of its GNP; and the average in Subsaharan Africa was 82 percent of GNP. The impacts are devastating. Unemployment has skyrocketed as farmers are forced off public lands and domestic economies are dismantled. Per capita income in the South has dropped to the pre-independence levels of the 1960s. Bread and gasoline riots are becoming commonplace in many Southern cities. Communicable diseases such is cholera, yellow fever, malaria, bubonic plague and pneumonia have increased as urban sanitation and infrastructure have deteriorated as public spending collapsed.[68]

When no more money or exports can be squeezed from the poor, selling state-owned companies to Northern corporations becomes an option. Privatization of public agencies totaled $30 billion in 1990,

They no longer use bullets and ropes. They use the World Bank and the IMF.

Jesse Jackson, Liberville, Gabon, May 1993

$88 billion in 1996, and $100 billion in 1997. The dollar estimates are almost meaningless, since the companies are often sold at bargain prices under duress. Once again, a handful of multinational corporations are the beneficiaries.[69]

Structural adjustment proved to be such a useful tool for leveraging corporate power that it was time to make it a permanent part of the global economy, and that is just what the international trade treaties of the 1990s have done—codified the elements of structural adjustment into international law.

"Free trade agreements" are not free, and are not primarily about trade. The major impact of the North American Free Trade Agreement (NAFTA) in 1994, the GATT Uruguay Round in 1995, and agreements under the World Trade Organization since 1995 is to force every country into full dependence on an unstable global economy dominated by Northern corporations and manipulated by "international" financial institutions interlocked with those corporations. Trade agreements have "liberalized markets" and "opened economies" by abolishing tariffs that protected domestic industries, removing financial controls that protected the public, and nullifying national and local environmental, health, and safety laws that protected people.[70]

- The treaty negotiations are dominated and manipulated by the richest nations, and the trade bodies are dominated by corporate lobbyists and lawyers.
- Agreements have been negotiated through secret and "fast-track" processes in which national legislatures must accept the entire agreement without amendment—often without even knowing what the agreements contain.[71]
- Entry into the World Trade Organization and other trade treaties is often conditioned upon additional structural "reforms" that destroy whatever independence might be left.
- Recent trade treaties enforce their provisions and control the policies of signatory nations by imposing trade sanctions, fines, and other penalties for violations. The richest nations can afford to chose which provisions they will observe.
- Unelected panels of trade officials adjudicate trade disputes, with the authority to have local and national laws protecting human rights, labor, consumers, and the environment struck down as "non-tariff barriers to trade" *(see profile on World Trade Organization in Part 2).*

International trade also encourages the "dumping" of goods overseas at less than cost. In order to eliminate competition, or to get rid of surplus production without destroying prices in the home country, multinational corporations (aided by their governments' agricultural and "foreign aid" policies) regularly dump grain, minerals, and other commodities at a fraction of their real cost. The purpose may be to eliminate competition or surplus products, but the effect is often to destroy local economies, ecological diversity, and social and economic diversity and self-sufficiency. NAFTA's opening of Mexico to cheap U.S. corn will force a million Mexican farmers off their land. The Mexican paper industry has been gutted by the enforced import of U.S. paper. "Capital" (corporations) and "financial markets" (investors) are freed to roam the earth unhindered while labor, consumers, and local businesses have to compete with subsidized multinational corporations.

POLICE AND MILITARY POWER: THE ULTIMATE WEAPON

As journalist John MacArthur pointed out in his book *The Selling of Free Trade*, "even in the degraded political culture of late twentieth century America, money still can't buy everything."[72] When advertising and propaganda, buying politicians, writing laws, controlling regional economies, and negotiating international trade treaties are not enough, corporate power uses its ultimate weapon: the police power of the state.

In the United States, the National Guard was established as a tool to control civil unrest and labor strikes,[73] but police and military actions against workers and citizens are a worldwide phenomena. Every year, hundreds of trade unionists are killed for organizing unions. Tens of thousands are fired, harassed, arrested, and tortured. It is estimated that ten percent of the U.S. workers campaigning for unions are illegally fired. Millions of men, women, children, and prisoners are forced to work against their will.[74]

Police are used to protect corporate facilities and the property and profits accumulated by the wealthy. Police are often hired in their off-duty hours to protect corporate property, making it difficult to tell the difference between public and private police. The unemployed are controlled by routine police harassment and brutality in the ghettos. During the 1990s, the U.S. prison population increased by 75 percent to two million inmates, two-thirds of which are black or Hispanic. Prisons are being privatized like many other public functions, and multibillion-dollar corporations are being subsidized with contracts for cheap prison labor.[75]

War is the continuation of politics by other means.

Prussian military strategist Karl von Clausewitz, who advocated total war against armies, civilians, and private property.

On an international level, governments have long engaged in diplomatic, police, and military action to protect the overseas investments of corporations. Restructuring local economies has been one of the primary prerequisites since colonial times.[76]

For example, British consular arrangements in Africa in the mid-1800s changed local property rules to benefit the colonial trade. In 1838, the Ottoman Empire, already weakened by capitulation treaties going back to the 1500s, was opened to European goods and investment by the lowering of tariff and non-tariff barriers to trade and by railroad, port, mining, and banking concessions to European corporations. Disputes were to be resolved according to the dominant government's rules.[77] These are the same methods now imposed in the Structural Adjustment Programs of the International Monetary Fund.

If treaties and trade agreements undermine local law altogether, social unrest follows, and may lead to direct intervention by the foreign power; some European colonies in Asia and Africa were created this way. The British "opium wars" in the late 1830s and early 1940s forced China to open its markets to foreign goods by accepting the establishment of free trade "treaty ports" in Hong Kong, Canton, Shanghai, and other cities.[78] British and American gunboat diplomacy in the nineteenth century resulted in control of various parts of Latin America, and treaties between Britain and the U.S. divided up the resulting resources and markets. Treaties between Britain and the U.S. in 1846 and 1850 led to the construction of the Panamanian Railway and U.S. military intervention to protect it, and provided for joint Anglo-American access and control of routes across Panama.

When gunboat diplomacy did not work, the colonial powers simply annexed territories as formal colonies or as "protectorates." In 1911, American military forces occupied Cuba and the U.S. Congress made Cuba a U.S. "protectorate" under the Platt Amendment. The (unratified) Knox-Castrillo Treaty of 1911 provided for U.S. loans to Nicaragua—and for the right of the U.S. to protect its "interests" in Nicaragua. U.S. Marines soon seized railroads and cities, and U.S. financial agents took over collection of trade revenues and the national bank and railways.

Politics is the continuation of war by other means.

American poet Thomas McGrath,
blacklisted as a communist in the 1950s.

In the 1950s, the U.S. Central Intelligence Agency was involved in the military overthrow of the elected government of Guatemala on behalf of the United Fruit Company (now Chiquita). The CIA supplied helicopters, fighter planes, Soviet-marked guns, and mercenaries, hid its weapons deliveries and spying under cover of front corporations, and fed the *New York Times* and other news media false information.[79]

PROTECTING CAPITAL AND FIGHTING FOR RESOURCES

The ethnic and religious elements of war are often the most highly publicized, but wars are fought to control strategic routes, to open markets, and to gain access to natural resources.[80] Religious and racial animosities were inflamed and promoted by the colonial powers for their own economic purposes, and today's corporations and their governmental allies are doing the same. For example, the African civil wars funded with profits from diamonds are also fueled by the superpowers, and the recent ban on "illicit" diamonds conveniently prolongs the global diamond cartel of DeBeers.[81] Since the late nineteenth century, the most valuable natural resource is oil.[82] Oil wars have been and are being fought in the Middle East, in Central Asia, in Latin America, and elsewhere.

Multinational oil corporations including British Petroleum, Occidental, Shell, Total, and Triton have signed contracts with the Colombian military and national police to fund the protection of their oil pipelines. Under the 1991 Special Contribution for the Reestablishment of Public Order, oil industry contributions to the war tax were scheduled to reach $250 million in 1996, and that year the Colombian government imposed a one-time surtax to raise $400 million to pay for additional security for oil installations. The oil corporations also provide "in-kind assistance [which] includes vehicles, health services and instruments, installations, troop transport, and helicopter flights. Cash payments are earmarked for security equipment, administration, communication, personal services, welfare upkeep, and a network of informants."[83] Occidental and the major U.S. weapons manufacturers lobbied for $1.3 billion in U.S. taxpayer monies, which was approved for military aid to Colombia in the summer of 2000 *(see also the profile of the U.S. Export-Import Bank in Part 2)*.[84]

You can't mine coal without machine guns.

> *Banker and industrialist Richard K. Mellon, in testimony*
> *before the U.S. Congress, June 14, 1937. His father Andrew*
> *Mellon was U.S. Secretary of the Treasury from 1921-29.*

The Balkans are known for long-standing animosities and periodic ethnic wars—some of which have been fueled for more than a century by the region's strategic location vis a vis the oil reserves of Central Asia and the Middle East. For the multinational corporations working alongside the North Atlantic Treaty Organization (NATO), one of the most important rewards for the recent "pacification" of Bosnia-Herzegovina will be the construction of a trans-Balkan pipeline to bring oil from the Caspian Sea region to Europe. William Ramsay, U.S. Deputy Assistant Secretary of State for Energy, Sanctions and Commodities, claiming that that Caspian oil is "crucial to the world energy balance over the next 25 years," has revealed that "there already exists a kind of outline of a new Silk Road running through the Caucasus and beyond the Caspian. We think oil and gas pipelines, roads, railways and fiber optics can make this 21st century Silk Road a superhighway linking Europe and Central Asia."[85] The European Union, the U.S. government, and a gang of multinational corporations (including BP, Amoco, Exxon, Unocal, Caterpillar, Halliburton/Brown & Root, and Mitsubishi) are using all the military, political, and economic tools at their disposal to destroy and recreate the infrastructure and economy of southeastern Europe in their own image. The conflicts of interest between government officials and corporate executives are blatant and revealing *(see profile of NATO in Part 2)*.

Public armies protect corporations, corporations fund armies, armies and multinational construction companies work together to destroy and then rebuild the latest political hot spots. War is waged by private armies as well. Journalist Ken Silverstein has found that "with little public knowledge or debate, the [U.S.] government has been dispatching private companies—most of them with tight links to the Pentagon and staffed by retired armed forces personnel—to provide military and police training to America's foreign allies. . . . A State Department official told me he could provide very little information even on background because of the need to protect the 'proprietary information' of the companies involved."

- Washington D.C. consulting firm Booz-Allen & Hamilton, in conjunction with the U.S. Navy and Marine Corps, runs the Saudi

---

There is plenty of law at the end of a nightstick.

> *Grover Whalen, corporate showman and New York City*
> *police commissioner from 1929 to 1931 during anticommunist*
> *"Red Squads" suppressing public demonstrations against*
> *unemployment (*New York Daily News, *March 7, 1930).*

Armed Forces Staff College, while O'Gara Protective Services (former U.S. CIA and Secret Service agents) protects the Saudi royal family and their property and provides Saudi forces with security training.

- Betac, a company under contract with the CIA, works closely with the Pentagon's Special Operations Command, which engages in covert activities in the Third World. Betac trains police in Latin America and provides U.S. corporate clients with "internal security."
- Military Professional Resources Inc. of Alexandria Virginia has been training Croation army troops since 1995, received $400 million from Saudi Arabia, Kuwait, Brunei, and Malaysia to train armies in Bosnia, and is expanding into Africa.
- The U.S. Defense Intelligence Agency sponsored a closed-door symposium in June 1997 entitled "The Privatization of National Security Functions in Sub-Saharan Africa."[86]

THE MILITARY AS INDUSTRY

While naked military force is (at least ostensibly) avoided whenever possible, the dominant nations are constantly engaged in military actions around the world.[87] The corporate economy and the military are codependent, and the military has become an integral and permanent part of the global (and especially the U.S.) economy.

In 1995, the U.S. spent $264 billion on the military, representing forty percent of the world's total military spending. The NATO allies of the U.S. spent another $148 billion that year, while the "rogue" nations (Iraq, Iran, North Korea, Libya, and Cuba), which are such a "threat" to U.S. (actually corporate) interests, spent a combined total of $9 billion.[88] This suggests that military spending is economic as much as military, and indeed, a quarter of the U.S. gross domestic product is military-related.[89]

The U.S. government subsidizes corporations that sell weapons to foreign governments. Between 1990 and 1996, foreign weapons sales negotiated by U.S. corporations and by the U.S. government itself totaled $98 billion.[90] In 1999, the federal government gave at least

---

In the councils of government, we must guard against the acquisition of unwarranted influence, whether sought or unsought, by the military-industrial complex. The potential for disastrous rise of misplaced power exists and will persist.

U.S. President Dwight Eisenhower,
farewell address, January 17, 1961

$7.6 billion in direct grants, subsidies, and tax breaks to corporations that exported weapons.[91] The U.S. government has stockpiled over $1.5 billion in grants and subsidized loans that U.S. firms can use to finance arms sales to Poland, Hungary, and the Czech Republic (the three new members of NATO). Estimates of the eventual costs of NATO expansion to U.S. taxpayers range from $400 million to $250 billion.[92] The U.S. Export-Import Bank also provides subsidies for military sales *(see profile of the Export-Import Bank in Part 2)*.

There is no way in which a country can satisfy the craving for absolute security, but it can bankrupt itself morally and economically in attempting to reach that illusory goal through arms alone.

Dwight D. Eisenhower

SYNERGY:
THE WEB OF POWER

The processes of corporate power do not work in isolation. The economic and legal mechanisms that allow the privatization of the commonwealth, externalization of costs, predatory economic practices, political influence-buying, manipulation of regulation and deregulation, control of the media, propaganda and advertising in schools, and the use of police and military forces to protect the property of the wealthy — all of these work synergistically to weave a complex web of power.

Activists have dedicated lifetimes of necessary work to deal with the results of corporate power, by trying to mitigate the results of power: an ever-increasing disparity in wealth and power and continual economic, political, environmental, and human rights crises.[93] For social justice campaigns to be strategic, it is also necessary to examine how privatization, externalization, monopoly, and other corporate power processes have been institutionalized. This institutionalization is exemplified in the structural adjustment programs of the World Bank and International Monetary Fund, and in recent "free" trade agreements which have culminated in the creation of the World Trade Organization. An understanding of such institutions provides a necessary tool for achieving the long-term goals of environmental sustainability and social justice.

We shall have world government whether or not we like it. The only question is whether world government will be achieved by conquest or consent.

Investment banker and U.S. intelligence officer
James P. Warburg, Washington, DC February 17, 1950

2

PROFILES OF CORPORATE POWER

PROFILES OF
CORPORATE POWER

In this section of the book, some of the major institutions of corporate power are described. The list may seem biased towards U.S. and European organizations, but those are the centers of corporate power. Although there is some competition for funding, prestige, and power, especially among the smaller organizations, the main characteristic of the groups is a consensus to promote corporate power at the expense of government and civil society. A careful reading will begin to reveal an informal division of labor among groups that are largely in consensus on the major issues.

The profiles include basic information such as address and website, the organization's mission, details about membership, structure, budgets, meetings, and miscellaneous anecdotes that help to reveal each organization's influence and its promotion of corporate power.

The key to the right appears with the profiles in this part and summarizes basic information about each. Thus, the key allows the reader to more easily compare different institutions as to whether they are U.S. or international, governmental or non-governmental, for profit or non-profit, and their approximate annual revenue. Each dollar sign represents $10 million in revenue.

U.S. Based	Ⓤ
International	Ⓘ
Governmental	Ⓖ
Non-Governmental	Ⓝ
Profit	Ⓟ
Non-Profit	Ⓟ
Upward of $30 million/year	$
$20 to $30 million/year	$
$10 to $20 million/year	$
Less than $10 million/year	$

NAME OF THE ORGANIZATION

AMERICAN ENTERPRISE INSTITUTE

1150 SEVENTEENTH STREET NW
WASHINGTON DC 20036
P 202.862.5800
F 202.862.7177
WWW.AEI.ORG

The American Enterprise Institute is a think-tank founded in 1943 which promotes "free markets, free trade, a vigilant defense, and individual freedom and responsibility."[94] AEI is "dedicated to preserving and strengthening the foundations of a free society—limited government, competitive private enterprise, vital cultural and political institutions, and vigilant defense—through rigorous inquiry, debate, and writing."

AEI has 50 resident scholars who write books, articles, reports and a magazine, *The American Enterprise*. These publications are distributed to government officials and legislators, business executives, journalists and academics. AEI also has more than 100 "adjunct scholars" at universities and policy institutes in the U.S. and abroad, and claims it is "cited and reprinted in the national media more often than those of any other think tank."

AEI claims it is "strictly nonpartisan and takes no institutional positions on pending legislation or other policy questions," but AEI scholars testify before congressional committees and advise all branches of government.

AEI is governed by 26 trustees including corporate insider and Vice President Dick Cheney and executives from major corporations including State Farm Insurance, Motorola, American Express, Enron, Alcoa, Kohlberg Kravis Roberts, and Dow Chemical.[95] AEI officers include Samuel P. Huntington (Harvard professor, member of National Security Council, architect of forced urbanization in Vietnam, author of Trilateral Commission report on "excess democracy"), former U.S. Senator Daniel Patrick Moynihan and economist Murray L. Weidenbaum, architect of deregulation under Reagan.

AEI is a tax-exempt non-profit organization with income of more than $19 million in 1998. Foundations provided 42 percent, corporations donated 28 percent, individuals donated 23 percent, and the rest came from conferences, sales, investments. Research, publishing, and conferences accounted for more than 75 percent of 1998 expenses. About 40 percent of research expenditures went for economic policy studies, and the balance was evenly divided between social and political studies and foreign policy and defense studies.[96]

AEI and the Brookings Institution operate a Joint Center for Regulatory Studies (JCRS) with the purpose of holding lawmakers and regulators "accountable for their decisions by providing thoughtful, objective analyses of existing regulatory programs and new regulatory proposals." The JCRS pushes for cost-benefit analysis of regulations, which fits with AEI's ultimate goal of deregulation.

The Joint Center's advisory board includes academics from Stanford, Harvard, MIT and other universities. The Center's work features legal and economic luminaries such as Philip K. Howard, Vice Chairman of Covington & Burling, where he serves as a senior corporate adviser and strategist focusing on mergers and acquisitions and provides regulatory and litigation advice. Howard is the author of *The Death of Common Sense: How Law Is Suffocating America* and contributes op-ed pieces to the *Wall Street Journal* and the *New York Times*. He advised U.S. Vice President Al Gore on his "Reinventing Government" initiatives, and was an advisor to the U.S. Securities and Exchange Commission's Task Force on Regulatory Simplification in 1996 and 1997.

The Joint Center also sponsors the work of Maureen L. Cropper, a principal economist at the World Bank, professor of economics at the University of Maryland, university fellow at Resources for the Future, and member of the EPA's Science and Advisory Board. Her research delves into such areas as "valuing environmental amenities from an empirical and theoretical perspective," the "public preferences for saving lives at different times and among persons of different ages," and "valuing the health impacts of pollution in developing countries and with the economics of deforestation."

AEI pushes free-market principles and attacks what it calls "obsolete" regulation of the environment and health and safety, energy, transportation, and the banking, insurance and other industries. AEI favors privatization of public housing, Social Security, banking and telecommunications. AEI also examines global trade, and is concerned about how "trade liberalization is being jeopardized by the growth of protectionist sentiment and by efforts to condition trade agreements on harmonization of environmental and labor standards," and questioned "the practical significance of governmental trade negotiations and financial interventions" in the global economy.[97]

The AEI's New Atlantic Initiative seeks to integrate North American and European political, economic, and security institutions and expand the integration to Central and Eastern Europe. The AEI has created a "Senate Working Group" on Central and Eastern Europe, chaired by U.S. Senators William Roth (R-Del) and Joseph Biden (D-Del), which "aims to provide an arena in which members of the U.S. Senate can discuss transatlantic issues with ambassadors and other officials from Central and Eastern Europe."[98]

BILDERBERG

The Bilderberg is a private annual gathering for the politically and corporate influential. The Bilderberg has no formal purpose, but provides
a secure annual venue for frank discussion and consensus-building
among corporate and government leaders. The first Bilderberg meeting, in 1954, was organized by Joseph Retinger, Prince Bernhard of the
Netherlands, and representatives from Unilever, Harriman, Morgan,
Rockefeller, and other corporations.

Bilderberg meets once a year in May or June in a different location: Athens Greece in 1993, Helsinki Finland in 1994, Bürgenstock
Switzerland in 1995, Toronto Canada in 1996, Atlanta, Georgia USA
in 1997, Ayrshire Scotland in 1998, Sintra Portugal in 1999, and
Brussels Belgium in 2000. Attendance at Bilderberg is by invitation
only and is surrounded by tight security. Bilderberg is European-led
but attended by heads of state and businessmen from Western Europe,
the U.S., and Canada, as well as by media representatives sympathetic
to the establishment view. Until recently, attendance was off the record
"in order to encourage frank and open discussion."[99]

U.S. Senator Jacob Javits attended the 1964 Bilderberg meeting in
Williamsburg, Virginia, and received permission to publish a background paper explaining the origin and purpose of the Bilderberg
meetings, a list of the persons who attended the Williamsburg series,
and a list of the first twelve Bilderberg meetings. These were published
in the *Congressional Record*.[100]

Prince Bernhard was chairman until 1976 (when he was impli-
cated in the Lockheed bribery scandal). Lord Peter Carrington, former
British Foreign Secretary and secretary general of NATO, was Bilderberg
chairman from 1989 to 1998. The current chairman of Bilderberg is
Etienne Davignon, director of Société Générale de Belgique, Belgium's
leading holding company, Suez Lyonnaise des Eaux, BASF, ICL, Solvay
and Kissinger Associates.

Bilderberg has no formal membership, but many of the hundred-plus attendees return year after year. The core group consists of the chairman and a steering committee and an advisory group. Long-time members of the Bilderberg steering committee and advisory group include the CEO of Xerox, former members of the U.S. Department of State (including George Ball, William Bundy and Henry Kissinger), the former prime minister of Portugal, the former secretary-general of NATO, media baron Conrad Black, Vernon Jordan (director of many corporations), Marie-Josée Kravis (nee Drouin; Hudson Institute), David Rockefeller, Renato Ruggiero (former head of the WTO), Jack Sheinkman (former head of the AFL-CIO Amalgamated Textile Workers Union), Peter D. Sutherland (GATT, European Commission, Goldman Sachs, BP Amoco) and James D. Wolfensohn (World Bank) *(see Appendix 6 for a list of Bilderberg leaders).*[102]

Topics discussed at the 48th Bilderberg meeting held in Brussels, Belgium in June 2000 included the upcoming elections in the U.S., globalization and the "new economy," the Balkans, EU enlargement and the European far right.[103]

The following is a copy of a May 14, 1998 news release from the Bilderberg meeting in Scotland:

> The 46th Bilderberg Meeting will be held in Turnberry, Scotland, May 14-17, 1998 to discuss the Atlantic Relationship in a Time of Change. Among others the Conference will discuss NATO, Asian Crisis, EMU, Growing Military Disparity, Japan, Multilateral Organizations, Europe's social model, Turkey, EU/US Market Place.
>
> Approximately 120 participants from North America and Europe will attend the discussions. The meeting is private in order to encourage frank and open discussion.
>
> Bilderberg takes its name from the hotel in the Netherlands where the first meeting took place in May 1954. That meeting grew out of the concern on both sides of the Atlantic that the industrialized democracies in Europe and North America were not working together as closely as they should on matters of critical importance. It was felt that regular, off-the-record discussions would contribute to a better understanding of the complex forces and major trends affecting Western nations.
>
> What is unique about Bilderberg as a forum is (1) the broad cross-section of leading citizens, in and out of government, that are assembled for nearly three days of purely informal discussion about topics of current concern especially in the fields of foreign affairs and the international economy, (2)

the strong feeling among participants that in view of the differing attitudes and experiences of their nations, there is a continuous, clear need to develop an understanding in which these concerns can be accommodated, and (3) the privacy of the meetings, which have no purpose other than to allow participants to speak their minds openly and freely.

To ensure full discussion, individuals representing a wide range of political and economic points of view are invited. Two-thirds of the participants come from Europe and the remainder from the United States and Canada. Within this framework, on average about one-third are from the government sector and the remaining two-thirds from a variety of fields including finance, industry, labour, education and the media. Participants are solely invited for their knowledge, experience and standing and with reference to the topics on the agenda.

All participants attend Bilderberg in a private and not in an official capacity.

Participants have agreed not to give interviews to the press during the meeting. In contacts with the news media after the conference it is an established rule that no attribution should be made to individual participants of what was discussed during the meeting.

We are grateful to the *Washington Post*, the *New York Times*, *Time Magazine* and other great publications whose directors have attended our meetings and respected their promises of discretion for almost forty years. It would have been impossible for us to develop our plan for the world if we had been subjected to the lights of publicity during those years. But, the world is more sophisticated and prepared to march towards a world government. The supranational sovereignty of an intellectual elite and world bankers is surely preferable to the national autodetermination practiced in past centuries.

David Rockefeller, Speaking at the June 1991
Bilderberger meeting in Baden Baden, Germany.

BROOKINGS INSTITUTION

1775 MASSACHUSETTS AVE NW
WASHINGTON DC 20036
P 202.797.6000
WWW.BROOKINGS.ORG

Brookings Institution is a tax-exempt think tank created in 1916 as the Institute for Government Research by a group of business leaders and academics led by St. Louis timber and mining executive Robert Brookings, who later served on the War Industries Board. The IGR was founded to provide research and expertise to help restructure government agencies in accord with modern business methods, in order to promote administrative competence and government efficiency. During the Depression Brookings took on government and corporate research contracts. Renamed in 1927, the Brookings Institution established itself as a conservative think tank supported by industry and critical of the New Deal social programs, which were seen as replacing free enterprise with central authority.

After the Second World War, Brookings supported the Marshall Plan and an active U.S. presence in the world, and by the 1960s had a reputation as a liberal think tank, but Brookings income flowed from Rockefeller and Ford Foundation grants and corporate contributions. By the mid-1980s, in keeping with the Democratic Party and other "liberal" institutions, Brookings positioned itself back in the "center" of the political spectrum again. In the 1980s Brookings studies called for government budget cutbacks, corporate competitiveness, and national security. In the 1990s Brookings studies promoted market-based incentives to replace regulation, increases in military spending, and "free" trade. In 1995, Michael Armacost, a U.S. State Department official under Reagan, became the president of Brookings.[104]

Brookings' cultivation of its relationship with corporations is manifested in the Corporate Relations Program and in "The Brookings Council," which was created in 1983 "to engage prominent business and community leaders in the most important issues facing society today. By interacting with leading experts and decision makers, Council members enhance their understanding of current and emerging policy questions and test their own ideas and convictions. The Council's 250 members provide valuable intellectual leadership to Brookings and contribute over $4 million annually." The benefits of Council membership are pro-rated based on the level of support, with an annual donation of $5,000 being the minimum. The Director's Circle members donate $10,000 or more, the President's Circle $25,000, and the Chairman's Circle donate $50,000 or more annually.

Brookings has a staff of over 200, including resident scholars. These scholars produce hundreds of books and reports and participate in dozens of conferences through numerous divisions and projects, including a Joint Center for Regulatory Studies with the American Enterprise Institute *(see separate profile of AEI)*, the Center on Law, Economics and Politics, the Center on Social and Economic Dynamics, the Center on Urban and Metropolitan Policy and the Brown Center on Education Policy. Brookings' Presidential Appointee Initiative aims to help the nominees of the next administration, regardless of who is elected, and to "promote an agenda of pragmatic reforms."

Brookings board of trustees includes the corporate CEOs and directors of AT&T, Fremont Group (Bechtel), Booz Allen & Hamilton, Kissinger Associates, Human Genome Sciences, Inc., Johnson Capital Partners, State Farm, Aetna, Times Mirror, the Las Vegas Sun newspaper, Heinz Family Philanthropies, ARCO, Chase Manhattan, USAirways, Bank of America, Levi Strauss, as well as Robert S. McNamara (former president of the World Bank) and James D. Wolfensohn (the current president of the World Bank). Brookings trustees also include directors and trustees of foundations, hospitals and universities, including Johns Hopkins University, University of Chicago Law School, Harvard, Rensselaer Polytechnic Institute, the Carnegie Endowment for International Peace, the University of Pennsylvania, the Doris Duke Charitable Foundation and the Andrew W. Mellon Foundation.

Brookings' revenues in 1999 were over $28 million; its net assets were $225 million. Over a third of its revenues come from foundations (William and Flora Hewlett, Rockefeller), corporations and individual donations; another third comes from endowment income.

BUSINESS COUNCIL

888 17TH ST NW #506
WASHINGTON DC 20006
P 202.298.7650
WWW. BUSINESSCOUNCIL.COM

Founded in 1933 by U.S. President Franklin Roosevelt to strengthen ties between the U.S. Department of Commerce and corporations, the Business Advisory Council (BAC) began as a quasi-official organization of 150 corporate executives. When U.S. President John Kennedy's first Secretary of Commerce resisted the organization's role, BAC severed its formal ties with the U.S. government. Kennedy soon repaired relations with the renamed Business Council by sending government officials to meet with the Council and corporate leaders across the U.S., and the federal government continued to rely on the Business Council for policy advice and for recommendations for government personnel.[105] Meetings of the Council (attended by various government officials), were sometimes held at The Homestead, an old hotel in the Blue Ridge Mountains of Virginia.[106]

By the mid-1990s membership had grown to 299 current and former corporate CEOs, but the Council's role in promoting the corporate point of view in the corridors of power seems to have been eclipsed by new organizations such as the Business Roundtable and the Heritage Foundation.[107]

The influence of the Business Council on elected officials is reflected in comments made by Jimmy Carter at its December 1977 meeting. Carter told the assembled business representatives that if they encountered government action "that unnecessarily encroaches on your own effectiveness, I hope you'll let either my Cabinet officers or me know, and I'll do the best I can to correct it . . . If you let me have those recommendations, I'll do the best I can to comply with your request."

(quoted in Laura Anker et al.,
The Structure of Power in America, 1987)

BUSINESS ROUNDTABLE

1615 L STREET NW, SUITE 1100
WASHINGTON DC 20036
P 202.872.1260
WWW.BRTABLE.ORG

The Business Roundtable is a lobbying group of more than 200 corporate CEOs, founded in 1972 by the CEOs of Alcoa, General Electric, U.S. Steel, and other major corporations. The Roundtable's premise is that "chief executives of major corporations should take an increased role in the continuing debates about public policy." Believing that "the basic interests of business closely parallel the interests of the American people, who are directly involved as consumers, employees, shareholders, and suppliers," the Business Roundtable has a single objective — "to promote policies that will lead to sustainable, non-inflationary, long-term growth in the U.S. economy." To promote growth, the United States "must create the right environment for American companies at home and abroad" — ranging from the privatization of social security, limits on corporate liability and limits on public control of health care.[108]

The Roundtable was influential in the election of Ronald Reagan, in promoting Reagan's tax breaks for corporations and the wealthy and in the Republican takeover of Congress in 1994. In 1998, the Roundtable ranked as the seventh-largest lobbying organization in the U.S.; it spent more than $11 million that year, and Roundtable member corporations spend an estimated $100 million a year on lobbying Congress to lower taxes, deregulate, reduce corporate liability by limiting lawsuits against corporations, privatize Social Security and to prevent reform of the health care system (see Appendices 1 and 2 for lists of corporations and lobbying firms).[109]

The Roundtable's "single objective" is to promote policies that will lead to "sustainable, non-inflationary, long-term growth in the U.S. economy,"[110] and the Roundtable claims to advocate public policies that "foster vigorous economic growth; a dynamic global economy; and a well-trained and productive U.S. workforce essential for future competitiveness." But a Roundtable front group, USA*NAFTA, spent $10 million to help secure a free trade agreement which has cost hundreds of thousands of U.S. jobs (USA*NAFTA was allowed to set up an office in the U.S. House Ways and Means Committee conference room). Three years after NAFTA had been signed, the Roundtable (and the Clinton White House) urged patience, because "the full benefits of NAFTA will not be apparent for several years to come."[111]

The stated purpose of the Roundtable's task force on international trade and investment is to "develop positions on trade and investment issues to enhance the competitiveness of U.S. business in international markets." The task force seeks to "implement trade education programs to increase general awareness and understanding of the importance of trade to U.S. economic growth, support efforts for new trade agreements and encourage Congressional renewal of 'Fast Track' negotiating authority, work to achieve normalized commercial relationship with China [and] support trade and investment policies that help raise American and global living standards."

Boeing CEO Phil Condit happens to serve as chairman of the task force. Perhaps the Roundtable's interest in the China trade is linked to Boeing's plan to sell $120 billion in aircraft to China over the next twenty years. In 1997-98, Boeing gave political candidates $1.65 million, and in early 2000, Condit offered further financial support to U.S. Congressional members who would vote to grant most favored nation (MFN) status to China.[112] The Roundtable is spending $6 million on the MFN campaign and to have China admitted into the World Trade Organization.

Another member of the Roundtable's task force on international trade is Michael Bonsignore, CEO of Honeywell and chairman of the US-China Business Council. Honeywell sells half a billion dollars worth of instruments, metals, chemicals, and electronics to China every year, and the airplanes China buys from Boeing contain Honeywell instruments and parts. Bonsignore's testimony did not mention China's military interest in Boeing and Honeywell products —but he reiterated that Boeing and Honeywell (and the Business Roundtable, by extension) are "deeply committed" to the China market.[113] It seems business as usual takes precedence over human rights, campaign finance ethics, military preparedness and engagement and other considerations.

The centrality of the Business Roundtable was indicated in Part 1 of this book. The Roundtable's membership consists of the CEOs of more than 200 leading corporations.[114] In the early 1990s, 79 of the Roundtable's directors held 206 board seats in 134 corporations, and held the following interlocks:[115]

- 36 directors were also members of the Business Council
- 5 were in the Council on Foreign Relations
- 3 were in the Institute for International Economics
- 2 were in the Center for Strategic and International Studies
- 16 were on the Committee for Economic Development
- 7 were in the National Association of Manufacturers
- 7 were in the Council on Competitiveness
- 1 was part of the Brookings Institution
- 3 were in the American Enterprise Institute

In addition to the task force on international trade and investment mentioned above, the Roundtable has task forces on government regulation, civil justice reform and the environment.[116]

The task force on government regulation, headed by General Motors CEO John Smith, seeks to "improve the effectiveness of federal government regulatory processes" by requiring risk and cost analysis of all federal regulations, which would be based on "market incentives and performance standards."

The task force on "civil justice reform" is headed by State Farm Insurance CEO Edward Rust and CSX Corporation CEO John Snow.

The environmental task force (headed by the CEO of Eastman Chemical) seeks to "reform" the Superfund for cleaning up toxic waste sites in the U.S., shape the recommendations of the World Trade Organization committee on trade and environment and "lay the foundation for a new environmental management paradigm" that integrates economic considerations in the development of environmental policy.

CATO INSTITUTE

1000 MASSACHUSETTS AVE NW
WASHINGTON DC 20001
P 202.842.0200
WWW.CATO.ORG

The Cato Institute is a think tank dedicated to "promoting public policy based on individual liberty, limited government, free markets, and peace."[117] It was founded in 1977 by petroleum millionaire and libertarian Charles Koch and Edward Crane of Alliance Capital Management.[118]

The Cato Institute promotes deregulation, private property and privatization by publishing books, policy analyses, journals, articles and radio programs on education, drugs, trade, immigration, foreign policy and the environment. Cato recently published a study titled *How and Why to Privatize Federal Lands* that proposed auctioning off all public lands over the next 20 to 40 years. The report was co-authored by the executive director of the Political Economy Research Center, Terry Anderson, who serves as an unofficial adviser on natural resource issues to President George W. Bush.

Cato estimates that government regulation costs hundreds of billions of dollars, perhaps 10 percent of the total gross domestic product.[119] Cato consistently attacks government regulation and intervention, whether it be in the form of taxes or social welfare. Cato's ideological consistency has led it to publish exposes of government subsidies of corporations. Cato estimated that tax breaks and other subsidies cost almost as much as social welfare programs, and pointed out that subsidies corrupted both democracy and business, that they foster an "incestuous relationship" between government and industry, that they strain the federal budget and are "anti-consumer, anti-capitalist, and unconstitutional." Cato identified more than 100 government subsidies that cost $85 billion in 1985, and singled out Archer Daniels Midland as a particular recipient of wasteful subsidies.[120]

Cato sponsors an annual monetary conference, which has been attended by Federal Reserve Board Chairman Alan Greenspan and others from the regional Federal Reserve Banks, U.S. Treasury Secretary Lawrence Summers, International Monetary Fund First Deputy

Managing Director Stanley Fischer and Harvard professor Jeffrey Sachs, author of "shock therapy" economic restructuring programs.[121]

Cato's Project on Global Economic Liberty pushes privatization, deregulation and globalization, and says that "unilateral liberalization" is the most effective way to achieve economic growth.[122] A recent Cato book, *Global Fortune: The Stumble and Rise of World Capitalism* says "the critics of economic globalization are wrong. Capitalism has created a century of unprecedented prosperity and its spread is necessary to lift the world's poor out of poverty.... What the world needs is more market reform, not a retreat from globalization."

Cato opposes laws discriminating against gays. It promotes the legalization of drugs, and opposes censorship of pornography. Cato's opposition to government intervention led it to oppose U.S. military action in the Persian Gulf and Bosnia. But libertarian positions on various issues does not mean that the Cato Institute does not support corporate power. In the absence of civil authority, eliminating government regulation and government programs simply means that corporate power is unchecked.

The privatization of social security that Cato favors would mean a huge windfall for the stock market and the investment banks managing corporate stock and bond portfolios (Cato's study of Social Security privatization has been supported by funding from insurance company AIG, which manages privatized retirement systems[123]).

Cato applauds the recent "reform" of welfare in the U.S., but its report, *Facilitating Fraud: How SSDI Gives Benefits to the Able Bodied,* "explains how the federal government is handing out Social Security disability payments to individuals who are not disabled and have no right to receive them."

Cato claims that government recycling programs are encouraging waste, that the states should set their own pollution standards and that Superfund and other toxic waste laws should be repealed.

Cato "adjunct scholar" Steven Milloy was the Executive Director of The Advancement of Sound Science Coalition (TASSC) in 1997 and 1998. TASSC membership includes more than 400 agricultural, manufacturing, oil, dairy, timber, paper and mining corporations and associations, including 3M, Amoco, Chevron, Dow Chemical, Exxon, General Motors, Lorillard Tobacco, the Louisiana Chemical Association, the National Pest Control Association, Occidental Petroleum, Philip Morris, Procter & Gamble, Santa Fe Pacific Gold Corp. and W.R. Grace & Co — as well as the U.S. Lawrence Livermore National Laboratory. The Cato Institute has published two of Milloy's books, *Science Without Sense* and *Silencing Science*. Milloy's newspaper columns, which are published by major corporate media, attack scientists studying the global climate change, accuse the Consumers Union of being biased towards environmental protection and dismiss criticism of biotechnology as "little myths."[124]

In 1998, Vice President Dick Cheney (former U.S. Defense Secretary and chairman of the petrochemical and military construction corporation Halliburton) told a Cato audience what they wanted to hear: that U.S. military and human rights sanctions against foreign governments were counterproductive because they affected the profits of U.S. corporations.[125]

Cato employs 75 staff and has 55 adjunct scholars and 14 fellows, "many of whom are among the country's leading advocates of free markets and limited government."[126]

Cato's budget was $12 million in 1998 and $13 million in 1999.[127] Most of the funding comes from conservative foundations such as Sarah Scaife and John M. Olin.[128]

MEETINGS

Cato holds numerous meetings to disseminate the findings of its research and advocates policies which further its political and economic goals. A current list can be found on its website.[129]

CITIZENS FOR A SOUND ECONOMY

1900 M STREET NW, SUITE 501
WASHINGTON DC 20036
P 202.783.3870
WWW.CSE.ORG

"AMERICANS WORKING FOR FREE ENTERPRISE AND LIMITED GOVERNMENT"

Citizens for a Sound Economy (CSE) was founded in 1984 by libertarians David and Charles Koch of Koch Industries, who have also founded other think tanks such as the Cato Institute. CSE received almost $5 million from various Koch foundations between 1986 and 1990, and David Koch and several Koch Industries employees serve as directors of CSE and the CSE Foundation.

Although CSE has recently received its funding from the tobacco and sugar industries and from major corporations such as General Electric *(see chart on page 66)*, CSE describes itself as "hundreds of thousands of grassroots citizens dedicated to (1) free markets and limited government, and (2) the highest level of personal involvement in public policy activism. Through recruitment, training, and political participation, CSE has become an army of activists. . . [who] continuously recruit, educate, and enable new members to participate effectively in public policy debates. CSE activists serve as local leaders who recruit others to join the fight for free-market policies." CSE has local chapters in Alabama, Arizona, California, Florida, Illinois, Iowa, Louisiana, Michigan, New Hampshire, New Jersey, New York, North Carolina, Ohio, Oklahoma, Oregon, Texas, Virginia and Washington.[130]

DIRECTORS OF CSE AND CSE FOUNDATION

- David Koch, founder of CSE, director of the Reason Foundation and Cato Institute.
- Sarah Atkins, TAMKO Roofing Products, daughter of CSE founders Ethelmae and J.P. Humphreys.
- Wayne Gable, director of federal affairs at Koch Industries, president of the Koch Foundation.
- Robert Tollison, professor of economics and finance at University of Mississippi, advisor to the Progress and Freedom Foundation.
- Walter Williams, the John M. Olin Professor of Economics at

George Mason University, substitute host for *The Rush Limbaugh Show*, and director of or advisor to: the Hoover Institution, Institute for Research on the Economics of Taxation, Landmark Legal Foundation, Alexis de Tocqueville Institute, Reason Foundation, *Destiny Magazine* and Cato Institute.

- C. Boyden Gray, White House counsel to U.S. President George Bush, partner at the Washington DC law firm of Wilmer, Cutler and Pickering, clerk for U.S. Supreme Court Justice Earl Warren.
- Gordon Cain, Sterling Chemicals, Sterling Group Merchant Bank, director of Cato Institute.
- Joseph Fogg, merchant banking and investment firm in Westbury, New York, former managing director at Morgan Stanley, Republican Party activist, advisor to Empower America.
- Thomas Knudsen, president of Thomas Publishers, New York.
- James C. Miller III, senior fellow at the Hoover Institution, former director of the Office of Management and Budget (OMB) and chairman of the Federal Trade Commission under Ronald Reagan.
- Nancy Mitchell, Koch Industries, former Bush Administration official.
- David H. Padden, Padden & Company investment securities, director of the Cato Institute and founder of the free-market think-tank Heartland Institute.
- Richard Stephenson, Cancer Treatment Centers of America and several other health care, finance and real estate companies.
- Dirk Van Dongen, president of National Association of Wholesaler-Distributors and Republican National Party activist.

Founder	Amount	Year	Purpose
General Electric	$ 500,000	1998	
Publix Super Markets	500,000	1998	
U.S. Sugar Corp.	280,000	1998	fight Everglades restoration
Florida Crystals Corp.	280,000	1998	fight Everglades restoration
Emerson Electric	200,000	1998	
AlliedSignal	200,000	1998	
Johnson & Johnson	200,000	1998	
Sugar Cane Growers Coop of Florida	140,000	1998	fight Everglades restoration
Hetz	25,000	1998	tort reform
DaimlerChrysler	25,000	1998	tort reform
Dollar Thrifty Automotive Group	10,000	1998	tort reform
Huizenga Holdings	75,000	1998	tort reform
Exxon	175,000	unknown	global climate issues
U.S. West	1,000,000	unknown	telephone deregulation
Philip Morris	1,000,000	unknown	oppose cigarette taxes
Microsoft	380,000	unknown	limit federal budget for antitrust
Sarah Scaife Foundation	200,000	1999	
John M. Olin Foundation	270,000	1997-1999	for the work of the organization and a fellowship for James C. Miller III
Charles G. Koch, David H. Koch and Claude R. Lambe Charitable Foundations	4,800,000	1986-1990	founders and regular funders

Most of CSE's income ($4 million in 1991, over $15 million in 1998) comes from corporations and corporate foundations.[131]

CONFERENCE BOARD

845 THIRD AVE
NEW YORK NY 10022
P 212.339.0345
WWW.CONFERENCEBOARD.ORG

The mission of the Conference Board is to be a "non-profit non-advocacy organization ... to improve the business enterprise system and to enhance the contribution of business to society."[132]

The National Industrial Conference Board was "born out of a crisis in industry in 1916," when "declining public confidence in business and rising labor unrest had become severe threats to economic growth and stability," and a "bubbling political/industrial cauldron teemed with anarchists, socialists, progressives, liberals, conservatives, and splinter groups of all shades." The Board sought to "reduce tension between capital and labor and end the mayhem that was crippling industrial development." As a federation of eleven of the nation's most powerful industry associations, the Board "concluded that the time had arrived for an entirely new type of organization. Not another trade association. Not a propaganda machine. But a respected, not-for-profit, nonpartisan organization that would bring leaders together to find solutions to common problems and objectively examine major issues having an impact on business and society."[133]

The Board's articulation of a broad public interest function is contradicted by its first committee, which was dedicated to publicity, not research, and by one the founders' minutes of an early meeting, which included the following: "The conference was called with the object of discussing constructively and comprehensively the causes of the increasing strife between employers and their employees and the effect of the rapidly multiplying amount of restrictive labor and social legislation on the conduct of business."[134]

The focus on controlling regulation has been evident throughout the Board's history. At first the Board produced studies and recommendations for "industrial progress," which emphasized labor reform, but soon created committees on anti-trust legislation, taxation, public finance, and international issues. The Board currently works on government relations, tax reform, political action committees, and reform of social security and pension systems.

The Conference Board has been addressed by standing U.S. Presidents, including Kennedy, Johnson, and Ford, as well as by former or future Presidents Taft, Coolidge, Hoover, Eisenhower, Nixon, Reagan, and Bush.[135] Bill Clinton attended the 1991 meeting before announcing his candidacy for U.S. President.[136]

A measure of the Board's influence is seen in U.S. President Johnson's implementation of Board recommendations for changes in how corporate tax depreciation was calculated. For example, the resulting changes to the tax code in 1965 alone resulted in $700 million in tax breaks to corporations.[137]

The Board also helped mobilize for Word War I by offering the Wilson administration "the cooperation and machinery of the Board in facilitating the government's work with the manufacturers of the country." Wilson's cabinet-level Council on National Defense responded by requesting Board assistance in assessing the labor situation and in promoting uninterrupted production of war materials. The Board advised that strikes and lockouts posed the greatest threat, and Wilson appointed Board members to the agency that set out the government's war-time labor policies.[138]

After World War II, the President's Committee for Financing Foreign Trade, another corporate-dominated advisory board, asked the Conference Board to analyze the obstacles to making foreign investments.[139] In the 1950s, after "World War II had introduced humanity to the atom and business quickly saw potential for its peaceful application," the Conference Board held annual conferences to promote nuclear energy among industry and government agencies.[140]

Such boosterism continues. In 1991, the Conference Board held a North American Free Trade Forum in Acapulco, Mexico, attended by business leaders and the chief trade officials from the U.S., Canada, and Mexico.[141]

The Conference Board bills itself as "the leading business membership and research organization where you can gain cross-industry knowledge and share experiences and best practices with executives from more than 3,000 organizations in 67 countries. A not-for-profit, non-advocacy organization, The Conference Board provides objective business knowledge through the Consumer Confidence Index and the Leading Economic Indicators and our research, conferences, centers, and councils."[142] The Conference Board claims it is not a lobbying organization, just "the world's leading business membership and research organization."

"Does The Conference Board lobby on any issues? No. The Conference Board is a non-partisan, non-advocacy organization."[143] However, the Conference Board's Council of Public Affairs Executives (CPAE) sponsors meetings on "corporate public affairs and government relations" to provide a forum for corporate public affairs officers to "examine issues as they relate to their company's policies and procedures." Recent issues discussed included the politics of the federal budget surplus, the evolving politics of health care, the implications of tax reform, corporate PACs in a changing political environment and Social Security and pension reform—all specific legislative issues on which millions are being spent to lobby elected officials.

The CPAE meets twice a year in Washington, DC. Attendance is restricted to the corporate public affairs officers. The 35 CPAE members pay annual membership dues of $3,000. Companies represented at recent meetings include Microsoft, Kmart, Unilever, Pfizer, Honeywell, General Mills, Dow Chemical, General Motors, Schering-Plough, UNUM, DuPont, UPS, Gannett, Deere & Company, Rolls-Royce, Citgo Petroleum, International Paper, Eastman Kodak and Warner-Lambert.

MEMBERSHIP AND STRUCTURE

Members include executives from more than 3,000 corporations from more than 60 nations.[144] More than 150 CEOs address 12,000 meeting participants at the annual meeting. By the early 1990s, the Conference Board's budget exceeded $20 million.[145]

Past chairmen of the Conference Board have included the heads of Westinghouse, RJ Reynolds Tobacco, Proctor & Gamble, Standard Oil of California, Republic Steel, Chemical Trust Bank, Bechtel, General Electric, IBM, RCA, General Foods, Goodyear and 3M. Some of these executives have also served as U.S. Cabinet secretaries or in other governmental or quasi-governmental positions. For example, oil executive Alexander Trowbridge served as Johnson's Secretary of Commerce before leading the Conference Board in the 1970s, and long-time Conference Board president John Sinclair had been president of the Federal Reserve Bank of Philadelphia.[146] Morris Tabaksblat, Chairman of Reed Elsevier, former Chairman of Unilever, and the Vice Chair of the European Roundtable of Industrialists, is also Vice Chair of the Conference Board.[147]

Conference Board trustees include representatives of Bestfoods, Phillips Petroleum, JC Penney, Excel, Texaco, Martha Stewart Living, Fidelity Management and Research, Goldman Sachs, British Airways and Unisys.[148]

The Conference Board's Councils are "groups of senior executives who meet regularly to share information, ideas, and insights on relevant business issues. They engage in candid, off-the-record discussions with peers in other companies, industries, and, in some cases, other countries. Each of our more than 100 Councils charts its own course: selecting members, setting meeting agendas, and serving the interests and needs of the group. Only executives in member companies of The Conference Board may participate."[149]

The Conference Board's Centers are "executive forums that bring together management research, publications, councils, and conferences in the areas listed below. They are designed to keep you in front of the latest developments in management strategies and tactics in their areas of responsibility. Only executives in member companies of The Conference Board may participate." The Centers are the Global Center for Performance Excellence, the Global Corporate Governance Research Center, the Information Management Center and the Townley Global Management Center for Environment, Health and Safety."[150]

The Board opened Canadian offices in the 1950s and European offices in the 1970s, and as part of its effort to "help business in the global marketplace, works with organizations around the world, ranging from the Chambers of Commerce in Thailand and Hong Kong, the Confederation of Indian Industries, the Singapore Trade Development Board, the Irish Management Institute, the Turkish Industrialists' and Businessmen's Association, the Mexican Business Council for International Affairs, the Conference Board of Canada, Harvard University's Kennedy School of Government, the National Institute of Standards and Technology, and the Peter F. Drucker Foundation for Nonprofit Management."[151]

COUNCIL ON FOREIGN RELATIONS

HAROLD PRATT HOUSE
58 EAST 68TH STREET
NEW YORK NY 10021
P 212.434.9400

1779 MASSACHUSETTS AVE NW
WASHINGTON DC 20036
P 202.518.3400
WWW.CFR.ORG

The Council on Foreign Relations was founded in 1921 by "business-men, bankers, and lawyers determined to keep the United States engaged in the world," and "to provide insights into international affairs and to develop new ideas for U.S. foreign policy, particularly national security and foreign economic policy."[152] The CFR seeks to "cooperate with the government and all existing agencies and to bring them into constructive accord."[153] The CFR's website claims that it "is composed of men and women from all walks of international life and from all parts of America," but its membership is largely unchanged from its founders: white, male, and predominantly corporate in background and viewpoint.[154]

During World War II the CFR, with Rockefeller Foundation funding, brought together corporate and media executives, government officials and academics to strategize the national interests, war aims, and postwar plans of the United States. Five study groups were set up: Economic and Financial, Political, Armaments, Territorial, and Peace Aims, composed of government officials from the White House, the State and Treasury Departments, the Pentagon, intelligence agencies, Wall Street bankers and attorneys, major industrialists and selected representatives of the media.

Many of the CFR recommendations, which were kept secret until well after the war, were implemented by U.S. President Roosevelt and his Cabinet departments. The public position of the U.S. government called for freedom, equality, prosperity and peace, but in private, government officials in the CFR study groups were considering the territories crucial to the U.S. economy in terms of markets and raw materials, and minimally defined the "Grand Area" as the Western Hemisphere, the UK and the remainder of the British Commonwealth and Empire, the Dutch East Indies, China and Japan—though the ultimate goal would be global economic unification under U.S. leadership.

The CFR study groups analyzed the necessity for an economic recovery plan after the war which would finance the rebuilding of European markets for U.S. exports — which eventually became the Marshall Plan — and laid out plans for postwar institutions under U.S. and British control, including an international monetary fund to stabilize currencies, an international development bank to subsidize and insure corporate investments in undeveloped countries, and a judicial institution to maintain security ("settle disputes") in an age of rising nationalism among newly-independent colonies. In 1944 and 1945 these were established as the IMF, the World Bank, and the United Nations.[155]

You may join the CFR only by invitation, and although the CFR has 3,600 members, they are "nearly all current and former senior U.S. government officials who deal with international matters; renowned scholars; and leaders of business, media, human rights, humanitarian, and other nongovernmental groups" *(the current CFR officers and directors are listed in Appendix 7)*.[156]

The CFR seeks to "find and nurture the next generation of foreign policy leaders and thinkers," by bringing "outstanding younger scholars" onto the Council staff through several fellowships.[157] For example, in the mid-1990s, National Public Radio correspondent Anne Garrels spent two years in Russia as a "fellow" with the Council on Foreign Relations.[158] The CFR also has a Fellow for National Security Studies position, which is named after the ultraconservative weapons manufacturer and philanthropist John M. Olin. The CFR conducts study groups and sponsors roundtables, and produces books, articles, and editorial pieces for mainstream newspapers, television, and radio.

In the late 1980s, the CFR, with the support of Harvard University's John F. Kennedy School of Government, sponsored a Study Group on Privatization which explored the politics of and profit in helping countries around the world accelerate "loosening the ties that bind their enterprises to the apparatus of government." Members of the study group included consultants to the World Bank/IMF, United Nations Development Fund, U.S. Agency for International Development, and other multilateral institutions which promote privatization of public enterprises through foreign "aid," loans, and structural adjustment programs.[159]

Several CFR task forces are established every year to address issues of "current and critical importance to U.S. foreign policy." Upon reaching a conclusion, a task force issues a report, and the CFR holds "informative meetings" for CFR members and the press.[160] Recent task force reports included *Promoting U.S. Economic Relations with Africa, Financing America's Leadership: Protecting American Interests and*

Promoting American Values, American National Interests and the United Nations, Lessons of the Mexican Peso Crisis, and *Non-Lethal Technologies: Military Options* and *Technologies.*

- The Latin America Conference in May 2000 was addressed by Robert Rubin, former U.S. Treasury Secretary and current Chairman of Citigroup.
- Lawrence H. Summers, then U.S. Secretary of the State, and Peter G. Peterson, investment banker and former U.S. Secretary of Commerce, laid out "The Right Priorities for International Development" in a meeting in March 2000.
- Summers is a popular speaker at CFR, giving his opinions on "The Trials and Tribulations of a World Economy" (March 1999), on "Lessons Learned from Mexico" and on "The Importance of the International Financial Institutions of U.S. International Economic Policy" (February 1997). Summers and IMF director Michel Camdessus considered "the future international financial architecture."
- U.S. Trade Representative Charlene Barshefsky, U.S. President Bill Clinton, global investor George Soros, and World Bank President James Wolfensohn discussed the global economy.
- U.S. National Security Advisor Samuel Berger, U.S. Defense Secretary William S. Cohen, and the Joint Chiefs of Staff evaluated future defense policy for CFR audiences.
- U.S. Commerce Secretary William Daley, Egyptian president Hosni Mubarak, and U.S. Energy Secretary Bill Richardson addressed business opportunities in the Middle East.
- *New York Times* columnist Thomas Friedman, Microsoft Chairman Bill Gates, and Grameen "micro" bank founder Muhammad Yunus expanded on their recent books.

MEETINGS

The CFR holds an annual National Conference and seminars based on study groups and independent task forces in key cities around the country.

FOR MORE INFORMATION

Laurence H. Shoup and William Minter, *Imperial Brain Trust: the Council on Foreign Relations and United States Foreign Policy* (Monthly Review Press, 1977).

AVENUE HENRI JASPAR 113
B-1060 BRUSSELS BELGIUM
P 32 2 534 31 00
WWW.ERT.BE

EUROPEAN ROUNDTABLE OF INDUSTRIALISTS

Founded in 1983 by 17 industrialists led by Pehr Gyllenhammar of Volvo and two European Commissioners, the purpose of the European Roundtable of Industrialists (ERT) is to unify Europe under one economic system, which will "strengthen Europe's economy and improve its global competitiveness. The ERT believes that the interests of European industry, its customers and the communities in which it operates, will be best served by promoting competition and competitiveness on a European scale. Europeans can only solve their problems by closer cooperation, by developing the Single Market into a steadily more integrated economic system, and by drawing on the full potential of the single market to stimulate investment, to increase production and to create new jobs."[161]

ERT does not lobby on detailed legislation, but rather helps set the overall agenda for European unification. Lobbying is the function of UNICE, with which ERT has a formal relationship (*see profile of UNICE on page 107*). Over the years ERT has pursued:

- The legal unification that led to the 1986 Single Europe Act.
- Development of European infrastructure in order to facilitate industrialization and trade.
- European monetary union through a single currency.
- Pushing European "industrial competitiveness" by harmonizing laws to reduce barriers to trade.
- "Innovation" through deregulation, financial restructuring and educational "reforms," which ensure that corporations have access to a trained and "flexible" labor market.
- Bringing Eastern and Central Europe into the Union in ways that benefit Western European corporations.[162]

ERT enjoys close access to the EC Commissioners, and the actions of the EC to unify Europe have closely followed ERT's recommendations.

All of the agenda items listed above have been or are being implemented — to the benefit of ERT members.

For example, in 1991-93 ERT began running what it calls "management seminars" in Hungary, Poland and Czechoslovakia,[163] and ERT's Business Enlargement Councils (BEC) are meeting with senior government officials in Eastern and Central Europe to direct those governments' spending and decision making towards projects that benefit corporations. ERT member corporations head the BEC for each country (Shell heads the BEC for Hungary, Solvay heads the BEC for Romania, and Lyonnaise des Auix heads the BEC for Bulgaria). Unilever has divided Central and Eastern Europe with its "rival" Proctor & Gamble, and national companies in the region are going out of business as the multinational corporations take over.[164]

Another success for ERT has been the increase in public and private spending on European infrastructure to facilitate unification; spending is expected to total 400 billion euros by the year 2010. More than 150 projects have been completed or are underway, including the Channel Tunnel, a bridge between Denmark and Sweden, railroad and airport links and 12,000 kilometers of new roads. ERT helped the European Commission plan the so-called Trans-European Networks (TENs), and pushes for more funding and faster completion. The European Union pressured the Swiss government into easing regulations and repudiating national referendums that called for the reduction of highway traffic.[165]

ERT membership is "by invitation only and is personal rather than corporate," but all 47 members are the "chairmen and chief executives of large multinational companies, representing all sectors of industry, which have their headquarters in Europe and also significant manufacturing and technological presence worldwide." The member list as of June 2000 included the major corporations of Europe: Unilever, TotalFina, Fiat, Akzo Nobel, Royal Dutch/Shell, Norsk Hydro, Siemens, Bayer, Deutsche Telekom, BP Amoco and Bertelsmann. Wisse Dekker of Philips and Helmut Maucher of Nestle have served as chairmen of ERT. Maucher has also served as head of the International Chamber of Commerce (see the profile of the ICC on page 87). The current Chairman is Morris Tabaksblat of Reed Elsevier (formerly of Unilever). The current Vice Chairmen are Gerhard Cromme of Friedrich Krupp and Morris Tabaksblat of Unilever.[166]

ERT Members meet in plenary sessions twice a year to reach consensus on priorities, budgets, and the publication of ERT reports and proposals. The ERT Chairman, two Vice Chairmen and five other elected members form a Steering Committee which makes proposals to the Plenary Sessions. Working Groups on issues like education, employment, environment, competitiveness, the internal market, enlargement and taxation are chaired by ERT Members and staffed by experts from the ERT companies. ERT Members nominate press officers who help to coordinate ERT communications to national governments, EU institutions and the press.

The ERT "identifies the most important issues, analyses the critical factors and makes its views known to the political decision-makers at the national and European levels by means of reports, position papers and face-to-face discussions." At the European level, the ERT has contacts with the Commission, the Council of Ministers and the European Parliament. Every six months the ERT meets with the government that holds the EU presidency to discuss priorities. At the national level, each ERT member has "personal contacts with his own national government and parliament, business colleagues and industrial federations, other opinion-formers and the press. The ERT has close contacts with UNICE (Union of Industrial and Employers Confederations of Europe), the official representative body of the European business and industry world vis-à-vis the European institutions."[167]

ERT working groups include:

- Accounting Standards (currently headed by Air Liquide)
- Competitiveness (headed by Solvay)
- Criminality against Companies (headed by Philips)
- Enlargement (of the European Economic Union)
- Environment (headed by Renault, and dealing with climate change and sustainable development)
- Foreign Economic Relations (headed by Peter Sutherland of GATT, BP Amoco, Goldman Sachs)
- Employment, Industrial Relations and Social Policy (headed by Saint-Gobain)
- Pension Reform ("ERT believes that European integration and economic competitiveness are hindered by current public pension programmes")
- Taxation (headed by Unilever)[168]

ERT's Competitiveness Advisory Group (CAG) is its institutional link to the European Commission (EC). Modeled after U.S. President Clinton's Competitiveness Council, the CAG was created in 1995. CAG consists of ERT members (that is, representatives of specific corporations), three trade union representatives and government leaders, including Jean-Clause Paye, the former Secretary-General of the OECD.

Through written reports and lobbying of policy-makers, CAG promotes ERT's agenda, including expansion of infrastructure, expansion into Eastern and Central Europe, deregulation, trade liberalization, privatization, market-based environmental incentives rather than regulation, cost benefit analysis of social legislation and re-education of workers to provide a flexible labor pool.[169]

ERT chairman Morris Tabaksblat, in a speech at the European Business Summit in June 2000, explained that Europe is an "an insufficiently competitive environment, saddling companies with too high a cost base and too rigid rules," and this "has to be rectified—and fast." He warned that markets and new industries like biotechnology should not be regulated (except of course to protect intellectual property). He warned that "public acceptance issues could stifle the European biotechnology industry at birth." Political decision-making needs to be "streamlined" and develop "organically" as technology advances. "Frozen regulations and frozen attitudes will be swept aside by global markets." Tabaksblat's regret was that "before they are, they can do immeasurable harm" by "limiting [business] options and dissuading investment."

He warned that in the United States, "nothing less than a new world is forming, as the so-called new economy takes root," and urged European business leaders to "shape up" and compete in order to "overtake the United States in a decade." Likewise, European policy-makers (the ones in government) needed to create "a business friendly environment, mainly by "eliminating red tape," and through "reform of the European social model."

Idealizing the accumulation of wealth, "from Venetian traders to the Dutch entrepreneurs of the Golden Age, from English mill owners to the German industrial dynasts," Tabaksblat declared that "there is nothing innately shameful about becoming rich, or emulating others who do, nothing un-European about it!" Better to "refashion the social conquests of the last new economy," by reforming the educational system in order to train and retrain the labor force for new jobs and by "injecting appreciation of the opportunities in change."

Tabaksblat pointed to the fact that more people in the U.S. (74 percent) have jobs than in Europe (61 percent), and urged that Europe catch up by getting more Europeans to work—including women, older workers, and young people. The fastest way to the future is to guarantee "adequate rates of return" and "easy access to markets and to capital." Change would be painful for many, and that "not least for unions specifically representing old trades and skills, for local communities where these trades have traditionally been carried out—this is difficult to digest; for Europe's policy-makers, however, it's time it was obvious." The "urgency" to win the "global game" by accelerating economic and social change is "out of your hands, as it is out of mine; timing is determined by the pace of change—in markets, in technologies, in expectations; we haven't the option to think some more about it—we've done that too long."[170]

HERITAGE
FOUNDATION

214 MASSACHUSETTS AVE NE
WASHINGTON DC 20002
P 202.546.4400
WWW.HERITAGE.ORG

The Heritage Foundation, founded in 1973 with funding from ultra-conservative sources including Scaife and Coors, is a think tank whose mission is "to formulate and promote conservative public policies based on the principles of free enterprise, limited government, individual freedom, traditional American values, and a strong national defense." Heritage produces articles, lectures, conferences and briefings for Congress, Congressional staff, executive branch policymakers, the news media and academia.

U.S. House Speaker Newt Gingrich called the Heritage Foundation "the most far-reaching conservative organization in the country in the war of ideas," and U.S. House Majority Leader Dick Armey said "when conservatives on Capitol Hill are looking to turn ideas into legislation, the first place they go is The Heritage Foundation." Two-thirds of the Heritage Foundation's 1981 policy recommendations to President Reagan were adopted.[171]

During the first session of the 106th Congress, Heritage experts briefed 143 Representatives and 41 Senators on issues ranging from taxation to ballistic missile defense, and held 72 working group meetings and issue briefings for congressional staff. In addition, 32 Heritage experts testified before congressional committees during 1999.

During 1999, more than 180 articles written by Heritage's analysts and executives were published in leading U.S. newspapers. Heritage analysts appeared on more than 125 television programs and nearly twice as many radio programs.

The Heritage Foundation's Center for Media and Public Policy was created in 1999 to help conservatives use the media more effectively, and to "increase the media's understanding of conservatives, conservatism, and the conservative approach to problem-solving." Heritage contacts reporters, columnists, editorial writers, news directors and broadcast producers, and organizes "fact-finding trips" so journalists "can see how problems are being solved nationwide at the local community level." The Center's national advisory board includes William F. Buckley Jr., conservative journalists Mary Lou Forbes, Paul Greenberg and Charles Krauthammer, and several professors of journalism.

Heritage Foundation programs in 1999 included:

- Governors Jeb Bush of Florida and Gary Johnson of New Mexico on school choice
- Ohio Treasurer Kenneth Blackwell and former U.S. Rep. Jack Kemp on tax reform
- Sen. Bob Graham (D-FL) on private construction of public schools
- Sen. Rick Santorum on the proper role of religion in politics and society
- Former U.S. Vice President Dan Quayle discussed foreign policy and national security
- Former U.S. Defense Secretary Caspar Weinberger discussed America's Cold War triumph
- Former U.S. Secretary of State Henry Kissinger and former CIA Director James Woolsey spoke in favor of missile defense.

Heritage urges rapid build-up of a sea- and space-based "Star Wars" missile system called for by the National Missile Defense Act of 1999, and calls for the U.S. to reject any restraint in the testing of nuclear missiles.[172]

Heritage takes predictable corporate positions such as attacking OSHA health and safety regulations and calling for the abolishment of the U.S. Dept of Labor, because it is "presenting a barrier to the formation of firms and their ability to create jobs."[173] Heritage wants to privatize social security, and says that states should have "flexibility" in their minimum wage, in order to help implement welfare reform, because the federal minimum wage is "a burdensome federal mandate that restricts [the states'] ability to help the poor."[174]

Heritage attacks labor's "leftward tilt" and says that "an activist labor movement may be the most significant new force in American politics, but the agenda of labor's new leaders is radically different from that of the traditional labor movement. Curiously, much of this new agenda is unconnected with workplace issues, not generally supported among rank-and-file union members, and clearly outside the mainstream of American politics. In recent decades, organized labor has been transformed from a relatively centrist political force into a powerful lobby for liberal special interests and big government. Organized labor has decided to use its billions of dollars in dues revenue to defeat conservative Members of Congress, while also encouraging the Boy

Scouts to admit homosexuals and atheists, offering financial contributions to political groups that promote abortion, and opposing welfare reform and a balanced budget."[175]

The Heritage Foundation's board of trustees includes archconservatives from the Scaife and Coors families. Richard M. Scaife is heir to the Mellon oil and banking fortune, and a board member of the Hoover Institution, Pepperdine University, and several family foundations, including the Sarah Scaife Foundation, The Allegheny Foundation, and the Carthage Foundation—all of which are funders of the Heritage Foundation.

Holland H. "Holly" Coors is a member of the Coors family, which was instrumental in creating the Heritage Foundation, and serves on the board of trustees of the Adolph Coors and Castle Rock Foundations. Joseph Coors is an honorary trustee of Heritage.

Other Heritage trustees include a former advisor to the U.S. Export-Import Bank, a former director of the U.S. Information Agency, a former Secretary of the Navy and the chairman of the conservative Amway Corporation, who also served as chairman of the U.S. Chamber of Commerce.

Heritage claims its more than 200,000 members make it "the most broadly supported think tank in America." Heritage Foundation had income of $43 million in 1998; two-thirds of it from individuals, 26 percent from foundations, and 4 percent from corporations. Amway, Joseph Coors, Pfizer, John M. Olin Foundation and the Sarah Scaife Foundation are recent funders of the Heritage Foundation's work.[176]

HOOVER INSTITUTION ON WAR, REVOLUTION AND PEACE

STANFORD UNIVERSITY
STANFORD, CA 94305
P 650.723.1754
OR TOLL FREE 1.877.466.8374
WWW.HOOVER.ORG

The Hoover Institution is a conservative think tank founded in 1919 as a center for advanced study in domestic and international affairs, supporting conservative scholars, sponsoring conferences, publishing books and articles, and producing television and radio programs.

The Hoover Institution says it "strives to conceive and disseminate ideas defining a free society, involving the study of politics, economics, and their interrelationships (that is, political economy) within the United States and other countries." The Hoover Institution describes its work in terms of the rule of law and property rights; promoting the idea of society based on individualism rather than classes; government performance in terms of accountability to society; economic growth and tax policy; and international rivalries and global cooperation with respect to security, trade and commerce, and the rule of law.[177] Hoover has a program devoted to the reform of public education, and addressing specific topics such as school curriculum, testing and standards, school finance reform, merit pay, the effects of teachers' unions, charter schools and school choice.

Government officials from the U.S. and overseas are invited to address Hoover Institution scholars, staff, supporters, and members of the Stanford community. Hoover researchers and staff give Congressional testimony, and offer what Hoover calls "public service" by serving as advisors to the U.S. government.[178] Hoover representatives also serve as missionaries overseas; the Hoover Library's deputy director, for example, serves on the editorial board of the International Democracy Foundation in Moscow.

Other Hoover scholars are former politicians. For example, former

Speaker of the U.S. House Newt Gingrich and former U.S. Secretary of State (and corporate insider) George Schultz are research fellows at Hoover. Other Hoover scholars include national security and Pentagon officials like William Perry, Richard Allen and Bobby Inman. "Honorary Fellows" include Ronald Reagan, Alexander Solzhenitsyn and Margaret Thatcher.

Hoover invites journalists to spend time at the Hoover Institution, "studying public policy issues in a scholarly environment, conducting research on topics of their choice, and interacting with resident fellows and visiting scholars."[179] The Media Fellows Program "has evolved over the past years to become a vital cog in the Institution's efforts to increase its impact on public policy discussion."[180] More than twenty media fellows were in residence at Hoover in 1998, influencing major newspapers (Los Angeles Times, New York Times, Wall Street Journal, Washington Post), magazines (Forbes, U.S. News and World Report, Newsweek, Reader's Digest), and television (ABC News, CNN's Inside Politics, and NewsHour with Jim Lehrer).[181]

The Hoover Institution produces its own mass media as well; its "Uncommon Knowledge" weekly TV series, produced jointly with KTEH, a PBS affiliate station in San Jose, California, is broadcast to eighty stations covering fifty-seven television markets in twenty-nine states.[182]

The Institution's annual budget is approximately $25 million. Like other ultraconservative think tanks such as the American Enterprise Institute, the Heritage Foundation and the Hudson Institute (see the separate profiles for these organizations), the Hoover Institution is funded by the ultraconservative foundations such as John M. Olin, Lilly, Smith Richardson, Carthage and Scaife.[183]

Forty percent of the Hoover budget comes from donations from individuals "and their related foundations and corporations." Another 45 percent of the budget comes from income from the Hoover's endowment funds, the market value of which exceeds $250 million. Another 15 percent of the budget comes from Stanford University,[184] which donated $4 million in the 1990-91 academic year. The Hoover Institution is a non-profit organization using Stanford University's tax exempt status, while the Hoover Library claims to be an "entirely independent" institution, even though it is located on the Stanford campus and Stanford accounts for about two-thirds of the Library's budget.[185]

Hoover's "board of overseers" includes the Archer Daniels Midland Chairman Dwayne Andreas, Texas oilman Robert Bass, Seattle television personality Jean Enersen, Herbert Hoover III, David Packard of military and electronics giant Hewlett-Packard, U.S. Secretary of

Defense Donald H. Rumsfeld, Mellon oil heir and ultraconservative philanthropist Richard M. Scaife and free-market guru and former U.S. Treasury Secretary William E. Simon.[186]

HUDSON
INSTITUTE

HERMAN KAHN CENTER
5395 EMERSON WAY
INDIANAPOLIS, IN 46226
P 317.545.1000
WWW.HUDSON.ORG

The Hudson Institute is a conservative think tank founded in 1961 by Herman Kahn, Max Singer and Oscar Ruebhausen. Under contract with government agencies ranging from the U.S. Departments of Defense and Justice to Wisconsin State to the City of Indianapolis, the Hudson Institute has published books and reports on everything from military strategy and national security, to agriculture and the environment, to trade, labor, and economic development, to health care, welfare, and education reform, but the primary focus is on "free" trade and enterprise and a strong military (founder Herman Kahn was a physicist and military strategist who suggested that nuclear war could be won). Hudson's annual awards have gone to such luminaries as Ronald Reagan, Dan Quayle, Barry Goldwater and Henry Kissinger.

Dennis T. Avery, author of *Saving the Planet with Pesticides and Plastic*, is the director of the Hudson Institute's Center for Global Food Issues. Avery "travels the country and the world preaching his gospel of biotechnology, pesticides, irradiation, factory farming and free trade." Avery claims that organic farming takes up too much land and thus destroys wildlife habitat, and that people who eat organic and natural foods are at a high risk for food poisoning. Avery's statements have appeared in the *New York Times*, *Las Vegas Review-Journal*, *Investor's Business Daily*, and the *Journal of Commerce*, and stories about "killer organic food" have appeared in the U.S., Canada and Europe, under headlines such as, "Organic just means it's dirtier, more expensive," "Organic food — It's eight times more likely to kill you," and "Organic food link to E. coli deaths." Avery receives a federal pension from his past employment by the U.S. Departments of State and Agriculture, and receives another $25,000 a year from the Hudson Institute. Hudson is funded by Monsanto, Du Pont, DowElanco, Sandoz, Ciba-Geigy, ConAgra, Cargill, Procter & Gamble, and other corporations.[187]

Hudson employs more than seventy researchers and staff and maintains offices in Indianapolis, Washington DC, Montreal and Brussels. In 1998 the Hudson Institute had a budget of $8 million, mostly from grants from conservative foundations such as Olin, Scaife and Pew (the president of the Hudson Institute is Herbert London, John M. Olin Professor of Humanities at New York University). Hudson is a tax-exempt non-profit organization and thus prohibited from substantial lobbying activities.[188]

INTERNATIONAL CHAMBER OF COMMERCE

38 COURS ALBERT 1ER
75008 PARIS, FRANCE
P 33 1 49 53 28 28
WWW.ICCWBO.ORG

US OFFICE
US COUNCIL FOR
INTERNATIONAL BUSINESS
1212 AVENUE OF THE AMERICAS
NEW YORK, NY 10036
P 212.354.4480
WWW.USCIB.ORG

ICC, founded in 1919, has thousands of member corporations and industry associations from over 130 countries. ICC membership is open to corporations and companies in all sectors, national professional and sectoral associations, business and employers federations, law firms and consultancies, chambers of commerce and individuals involved in international business. "By being part of ICC, members gain influence both at national and international level. ICC offers members many of the advantages of belonging to a prestigious club and the chance to forge business relationships at the highest level at exclusive ICC events."[189]

ICC claims to be "the world business organization, the only representative body that speaks with authority on behalf of enterprises from all sectors in every part of the world." ICC committees in the "world's major capitals coordinate with their membership to address the concerns of the business community and to convey to their governments the business views formulated by ICC." The topics of concern to ICC range from advertising and marketing, arbitration, banking, business in society, business law, commercial crime, commercial practice, competition, customs, economic policy, e-commerce, energy, environment, extortion and bribery, financial services and insurance, intellectual property, taxation, telecommunications, trade and investment and transport.

"ICC promotes an open international trade and investment system and the market economy. Its conviction that trade is a powerful force for peace and prosperity dates from the organization's origins early in the last century. The small group of far-sighted business leaders who founded ICC called themselves 'the merchants of peace'" and ICC "works for the liberalization of trade and investment within the multilateral trading system."

MAKING THE RULES, FORMAL AND INFORMAL

The ICC compares itself, with no apparent humor or irony, to an international government. "The ICC World Council is the equivalent of the general assembly of a major intergovernmental organization. The big difference is that the delegates are business executives and not government officials." As if proof that there is no need for another government, ICC states that "companies look to ICC as they meet the challenges of globalization and adjust to a world in which the state's role in the economy is no longer pre-eminent."

As long as it is ruling the world, ICC offers to act as judge and jury as well through its International Court of Arbitration, "the world's leading arbitral institution." The ICC shows others how to make the law as well, through its Institute of World Business Law, which offers courses and seminars to lawyers and corporate executives on everything from investment protection and negotiation of contracts to international arbitration.

"ICC members are at the forefront of business self-regulation. ICC is world leader in setting voluntary rules, standards and codes for the conduct of international trade that are accepted by all business sectors and observed in thousands of transactions every day." The rules include trading instruments such as Incoterms (ICC's standard commercial terms), the Uniform Customs and Practice for Documentary Credit and GUIDEC (a set of guidelines for ensuring trustworthy digital transactions over the Internet).

ICC members "establish the business stance" on trade and investment policies on financial services, information technologies, telecommunications, marketing ethics, the environment, transportation, competition law and intellectual property.

MAKING THE CASE FOR THE GLOBAL ECONOMY

"The great debate on globalization is in full swing. Can — or should — it be stopped? Is it pushing governments to the sidelines? Does it have a human face? Is it a threat to jobs? What are the benefits and what is the downside? ICC is convinced that the emergence of a global market economy, a process that has only just begun, will bring unprecedented prosperity to millions. But the right balance needs to be found between rules and freedom if the global economy is to realize its full potential. This is what this new section of the ICC web site is all about. We make the case for the global economy." ICC has made its case in a steady stream of articles, some of which can be read on the ICC website:

- Globalization Holds the Key to Ending World Poverty
- Free Trade Helps Developing Countries Catch Up

- Growth is Good for the Poor
- Victims of the Refusal to Globalize
- Multinationals are a Positive Force
- Globalization Offers a Road Out of Poverty
- Trade is Often the Best Way to Improve the Environment
- Globalization is Irreversible and Not an Option

SPECIAL RELATIONSHIPS WITH THE UNITED NATIONS AND WTO

"ICC's privileged links with major international organizations, including the UN and its specialized agencies and the World Trade Organization, allow the organization to effectively represent the interests of its members in international fora. ICC members prepare business positions for submission to international organizations and also, through ICC's global network of national committees, to governments."

"ICC works with the United Nations, other international organizations and regional bodies to ensure that they take the business viewpoint into consideration when making decisions affecting the private sector. It carries out collaborative projects with international organizations and provides business expertise to policy makers. ICC's permanent representatives on-site in Geneva and New York are responsible for relations with the UN and other international organizations."

"The United Nations: ICC is engaged in intensive dialogue with

---

Even when the proposed Multilateral Agreement on Investment (MAI) ran into strong opposition in 1998, business groupings like the International Chamber of Commerce (ICC) refused the OECD's proposals to include some rules for corporation behaviour. The ICC has campaigned vigorously against binding regulations in numerous multilateral environmental treaties, including those on climate change, biodiversity and ozone-depleting chemicals (the Montreal Protocol), promoting self-regulation instead. The U.S. Council on International Business (USCIB), the U.S. affiliate of the ICC, fiercely resists corporate codes of conduct promoted by trade unions and environmental and human rights organizations. In December 1998, the USCIB issued a statement saying that "Such externally imposed codes are unacceptable to the business community, are unworkable, and would be ineffective in resolving labour and environmental problems." The USCIB calls the demands made on business by NGOs "unrealistic, contradictory, and counterproductive" and rejects "the notion that companies can be held responsible for the overall behaviour and policies of their subcontractors and suppliers throughout the supply chain." The USCIB furthermore rejects the desirability of standardising corporate codes of conduct, and is vehemently opposed to the independent auditing and verification of "these imposed codes," warning against "the hazards of accepting such an intrusion."

Corporate Europe Observer,

Issue 5, October 1999

(citing PR Newswire, *December 21, 1998)*

the United Nations and its Secretary General on how business expertise can help the UN to attain its economic objectives." "Within a year of the creation of the United Nations, ICC was granted consultative status at the highest level with the UN and its specialized agencies."

"ICC enjoys consultative status at the highest level with the United Nations and its agencies. It is the preferred partner of international and regional organizations whenever decisions have to be made on global issues of importance to business."

"The World Trade Organization: At its regular meetings with ambassadors to the World Trade Organization, ICC is promoting business ideas and objectives for achieving a successful new round of trade negotiations."

LEADERS OF THE RICH NATIONS, ADVISING THE POOR NATIONS

"The Group of Seven industrial countries: Every year, the head of the host government of the G7 industrial countries confers with the ICC presidency on the eve of the summit. The consultation has proved to be a highly effective means of channeling business recommendations to the summit leaders."

"Guides to investment: In a joint project with UNCTAD, ICC enlisted support from 30 major companies in providing guidance to least developed countries on policies and practical steps to attract more foreign direct investment."

INVESTIGATING CRIME

ICC Commercial Crime Services investigates commercial crimes "committed on land, at sea or in cyberspace. . . Unencumbered by bureaucracy, and at the request of clients from the worlds of international finance, trade and transport, CCS multidisciplinary staff are in a unique position to respond swiftly to alerts anywhere in the world." "Investigations are carried out by CCS for commercial clients with a view to recovering losses. In addition, victims of fraudulent transactions are given help to extricate themselves and to minimize damage. Back-up services provided by the commercial crimes division of ICC include legal advice, support in litigation and expert testimony in courts of law."

The ICC International Maritime Bureau "covers all types of fraud and malpractice in trading and transport. In cases of maritime fraud or when ships fall victim to pirate attacks, the bureau reacts swiftly using staff and contacts worldwide. The bureau, which has observer status with Interpol, also investigates suspicious cargo losses from containers during sea, road and rail transits."

ICC's Commercial Crime Bureau investigates "financial frauds and suspected scams to enable recoveries to be made. In conjunction with the bureau's work to trace and recover assets, senior staff members can provide expert testimony at court hearings anywhere in the world."

ICC has a Counterfeiting Intelligence Bureau which traces fake products back from point of sale to place of manufacture. The ICC Cybercrime Unit identifies criminal interference on corporate computer networks. ICC showcased an "anti-piracy life-jacket," designed to protect sailors in case of pirate attacks, at the London Dome in June 2000. ICC's Piracy Reporting Centre found a hijacked tanker in South East Asian waters in June 2000, and now has a dedicated website where ship owners can log-on and view the exact position of their vessels at any time."

MEMBERSHIP AND STRUCTURE

The ICC consists of 5,500 corporations and 1,700 organizations (mainly trade and industrial associations and chambers of commerce), nominated by national committees or groups in more than 60 countries. The governing body, the ICC Council, meets twice per year. An executive board of fifteen to twenty members is appointed by the ICC Council. The member-wide Congress meets every three years, with the 33rd meeting held in Budapest in May 2000.[190]

OFFICERS[191]

- ICC President Adnan Kassar is CEO of Fransabank Group, a leading finance and banking group, with offices in Beirut, Paris, Hong Kong and Budapest. Kassar is president of the Federation of Lebanese Chambers of Commerce, Industry and Agriculture, permanent vice chairman and former president of the General Union of Chambers of Commerce, Industry and Agriculture for Arab Countries.
- ICC Vice President Richard D. McCormick is a director of United Airlines, Wells Fargo, United Technologies, and Concept Five Technologies, former CEO of US West, and Chairman of the US Council for International Business.
- ICC Member of the Presidency Helmut O. Maucher is a former CEO and Chairman of Nestlé, Chairman of the Council on European Responsibilities (COEUR), and board member of the Industrial Investment Council (IIC). Maucher completed two years as ICC President in December 1998.
- ICC Secretary General Maria Livanos Cattaui was previously with the World Economic Forum in Geneva, and was responsible for the annual meeting in Davos.

"ICC's programme of conferences and seminars is an essential channel for passing on the world business organization's expertise to a wider audience. ICC conferences are held in all parts of the world, many of them in collaboration with national committees." "ICC conferences are always highly topical and are often a platform for defining policies favourable to business."

"Every two years ICC holds its World Congress, always at a different venue and at the invitation of a national committee. These are major global business events that bring together business and public leaders to discuss issues that affect the environment in which they work."

"At the invitation of ICC Hungary, ICC's 33rd World Congress, 'The New Europe in the World Economy' was held on 3-5 May 2000 in Budapest. With the full backing of the Hungarian government, the congress was inaugurated by President Arpad Göncz of Hungary and ICC President Adnan Kassar. Its main themes were financial strength, the global view, the world trade agenda, big issues for companies and EU enlargement. Representatives from business and governments worldwide attended the congress, with a particularly strong participation from countries in the region."[192]

The U.S. Council on International Business is the U.S. affiliate of the ICC.

NORTH ATLANTIC TREATY ORGANIZATION (NATO)

BLVD LEOPOLD III
1110 BRUSSELS, BELGIUM
WWW.NATO.INT

NATO was established as the Atlantic Alliance in 1949 as a defensive political and military alliance between ten European countries, the U.S. and Canada. The stated purpose of NATO is to provide for the common security of its members through economic, scientific, political and military cooperation and consultation.[193] NATO "peacekeeping" activities have increased in the 1990s.

Recent NATO military action in Yugoslavia is part of a long strategic (economic) battle to control the Balkans and the Central Asian resources that lie beyond. The current focus is to secure oil and gas pipeline routes from the oilfields of the Caspian Sea to the consumers of Europe. Multinational oil corporations are signing multibillion-dollar contracts with Kazakhstan, Azerbaijan and Turkmenistan, while the U.S., European and Russian governments are lobbying, bribing, fomenting civil wars and conducting their own military operations in order to secure territory. Players include former British Energy Minister Tim Eggar (now CEO of the British corporation Monument Oil), former British Foreign Minister Malcolm Rifkind (now a director of British oil corporation Ramco), two former U.S. National Security Advisors, Zbigniew Brzezinski and Brent Scowcroft (now a director of AIOC), as well as former U.S. Secretary of State James Baker (oil corporation attorney), former U.S. Secretary of the Treasury Lloyd Bentsen, former U.S. Defense Secretary Dick Cheney (then CEO of oil services corporation Halliburton, now U.S. Vice President), and former White House chief of staff John Sununu. Iran-Contra figure and former U.S. Air Force major general Richard Secord has been helping to train the Azerbaijani army.[194]

NATO

Since the collapse of the Soviet Union in 1989 and the Warsaw Pact in 1991, Western powers have been moving economically and militarily into the vacuum. The U.S. brings weapons as well as oil technology. The U.S. government accounts for more than a third of the world's military spending, and the U.S. exports three times more weapons than Russia, its nearest competitor:

Top exporters of major conventional weapons, 1995-1999
(data in 1990 U.S. $ million) [195]

U.S.	53,443	Netherlands	2,239
Russia	14,628	China	2,212
France	11,731	Ukraine	2,048
UK	7,343	Italy	1,965
Germany	6,085	Canada	1,095

Weapons are manufactured by corporations, but much of the expense is funded by U.S. taxpayers. In addition, the U.S. government is a major promoter of the sale of weapons to other countries, and through its Departments of Defense, State and Commerce, probably has more than 6,000 employees spending $400 million a year to promote weapons exports.[196] The U.S. Commerce Department pushes arms exports by analyzing markets and finding buyers.[197] U.S. Secretaries of Commerce promote U.S. weapons sales as part of their overseas trade missions. The Secretary of Defense makes explicit sales pitches to foreign governments and negotiates sales contracts on behalf of specific corporations such as Boeing and Lockheed Martin. The U.S. government displays U.S. weapons, offers test flights and sends military personnel to air and weapons shows in Europe, Asia and Latin America. The U.S. ambassadors, in cooperation with U.S. manufacturers, push sales of U.S. helicopters, planes and missiles in the host countries.[198]

NATO has been restructuring its policies to "meet the new security challenges" in Europe by adding new members from Central and Eastern Europe.[199] The expansion of NATO is seen by U.S. weapons manufacturers as a huge new market for their products, and the U.S.

Do you want to know the cause of war? It is capitalism, greed, and the dirty hunger for dollars. Take away the capitalist and you will sweep war from the earth.

Henry Ford
(from interview in Detroit Daily News*)*

government is doing everything it can to help sell weapons. The Aerospace Industries Association, a trade association of weapons manufacturers, estimates that $10 billion in military aircraft may be sold to new NATO members such as Poland, Hungary and the Czech Republic. RAND estimates total weapons sales to Eastern and Central Europe may reach $35 billion in the next decade.[200]

Some of these weapons will be manufactured in Europe by partnerships between U.S. and European corporations. Boeing has acquired 35 percent of Czech aircraft manufacturer Aero Vochody. Textron bought 70 percent of Romanian helicopter manufacturer IAR Brasov. Lockheed Martin has agreed to build F-16 aircraft in partnership with the Polish manufacturer PZL Mielec. Some or all of the costs of these weapons is thus "offset" by U.S. corporate investments in European companies, by the resulting technology transfers and by U.S. corporate promises to promote the country's exports in international markets. One analysis estimated that between U.S. government subsidies and the transfer of U.S. jobs and sales overseas as part of European partnerships, the U.S. economy actually lost more than $1 billion on weapons sales in 1996.[201]

Boeing, Raytheon, United Technologies and TRW funded NATO's 50th Anniversary celebrations in Washington, and the host committee is made up of weapons corporation executives and former U.S. Commerce Department officials.[202]

The U.S. weapons industry routinely spends more than $40 million per year on lobbying government officials, and contributes more than $10 million to U.S. political candidates.[203] Weapons industry lobbying organizations include the U.S. Committee on NATO (formerly the U.S. Committee to Expand NATO), the Aerospace Industries Association, the American League for Exports and Security Assistance (ALESA), and the Defense Policy Advisory Committee on Trade (DPACT), a quasi-official group providing "advice" to the U.S. government. Weapons lobbyists also work with ethnic lobbying organizations. For example, the U.S. Committee on NATO works with the Polish American Congress and the Hungarian American Foundation, which are also working to promote NATO expansion.[204]

One of the ways the U.S. government promotes weapons sales is by making loans to the countries buying weapons from U.S. corporations. In the 1990s, $9 billion in loans were written off for various

Endless money forms the sinews of war.

Cicero, Philippics

political and economic reasons. But since 1995, the U.S. government has offered another $1.5 billion in grants, subsidized loans and weapons giveaways to prospective NATO members, and arranges test flights of U.S. fighter aircraft for potential government customers.[205]

Lockheed Martin received a $10 million grant from the Pentagon to coordinate a series of Air Sovereignty Operations Centers (ASOC) set up in Hungary, Poland, the Czech Republic, Slovakia and Romania.[206]

The U.S. Defense Export Loan Guarantee (DELG) program, created in 1995 after lobbying by U.S. weapons manufacturers, offers guaranteed loans on sales of U.S. military equipment to 39 countries, including 10 nations in Eastern and Central Europe. The U.S. Defense Department's International and Commercial Programs office works with bankers and weapons industry executives to promote the sales.[207]

Under the spur of profit potential, powerful lobbies spring up to argue for even greater munitions expenditures. And the web of special interests grows.

Dwight D. Eisenhower,
Waging Peace, 1963

RAND

700 MAIN STREET
PO BOX 2138
SANTA MONICA, CA 90407
P 310.451.6974
WWW.RAND.ORG

RAND maintains offices in Arlington, Virginia; Pittsburgh, Pennsylvania; New York City (Council for Aid to Education); and Leiden, Netherlands.

Project RAND (which stands for Research And Development) was originally set up during World War II by the Douglas Aircraft Company and the U.S. Air Force (then the Army Air Force) to analyze ways to improve the effectiveness of the B-29 bomber. After the war, the Commanding General of the Army Air Force, in a report to the Secretary of War, wrote:

> "During this war the Army, Army Air Forces, and the Navy have made unprecedented use of scientific and industrial resources. The conclusion is inescapable that we have not yet established the balance necessary to insure the continuance of teamwork among the military, other government agencies, industry, and the universities. Scientific planning must be years in advance of the actual research and development work."[208]

As a result, RAND became an independent non-profit corporation in 1948, "dedicated to furthering and promoting scientific, educational, and charitable purposes for the public welfare and security of the United States." RAND's original board of trustees included representatives of Douglas Aircraft, the president of Carnegie Corporation, the president of the California Institute of Technology, an attorney who later served as president and chairman of the Ford Foundation, the director of Westinghouse's research laboratories, a military consultant and a physicist from MIT, a social scientist from Princeton University, the president of the University of Illinois and the director of Battelle Memorial Institute.

The Ford Foundation, Pacific National Bank, Wells Fargo Bank and Union Trust Company arranged the initial financing. The U.S. government still provides the largest share of RAND's budget, but corporate foundations (Ford) and corporate clients also provide funding.[209]

Describing itself as "a nonprofit institution that helps improve policy and decision making through research analysis," RAND employs more than 600 researchers in economics, mathematics and statistics, medicine, law, business, physical sciences, engineering, social sciences, arts and letters and computer science. The staff comes from "the laboratories of industry, the seminars of universities, and the offices of administration, [and RAND] is very conscious of [the] need for teamwork."[210]

RAND research areas include space systems, digital computing and artificial intelligence, systems analysis, social policy planning, poverty, health care and education. RAND has compiled a comprehensive data base on AIDS victims, and analyzed the debate over class action lawsuits. One RAND report was devoted to *Identifying Policy Options for Developing Countries*. RAND's website explains how the diverse subjects are unified:

> "With roots in the Cold War competition with the Soviet Union, the early defense-related agenda evolved—in concert with the nation's attention—to encompass such diverse subject areas as space; economic, social, and political affairs overseas; and the direct role of government in social and economic problem-solving at home."[211]

RAND's "economic problem-solving" includes protecting corporations from liability for their actions. As RAND explains it, "The stakes are rising in the American system of civil justice. Hundreds of millions of dollars in liability payments as well as the international competitiveness of some of America's most influential corporations rest on the decisions of our nation's lawmakers. Not surprisingly, the work of RAND's Institute for Civil Justice on monitoring this system, analyzing procedures, and evaluating options for reform has gained national prominence."

Military research remains a key focus, and RAND enjoys a special relationship to the Pentagon. RAND research for the U.S. Secretary of Defense, the Joint Staff, the Unified Commands, the defense agencies, the United States Marine Corps and the United States Navy is carried out within the National Defense Research Institute (NDRI), a federally funded research and development center. RAND's Arroyo Center, founded in the 1980s, is the U.S. Army's only federally-funded research and development center for studies and analysis. Project AIR FORCE, an "independent" nonprofit research and analysis institution under contract to the U.S. Air Force since the 1940s, is a division of RAND. "[These military research] activities are complemented by RAND's domestic and international research on health, education, civil and criminal justice, labor and population, international economics, and science and technology."[213] For example, RAND projects "help policy-makers understand world political, military, and economic trends; the sources of potential regional conflict; and emerging threats to U.S. national security."[214]

In March 2000, RAND's Arroyo Center hosted an educational conference to discuss "the preparedness of the U.S. military to fight in the teeming streets of what may become the increasingly unavoidable battlefield of the future: the foreign city." Other studies have considered *Air Power as a Coercive Instrument,* and analyzed *International Law and the Politics of Urban Air Operations.*[215]

From its Arlington, Virginia office near CIA headquarters, RAND conducts research for the Central Intelligence Agency, the National Reconnaissance Office, the National Intelligence Council and other "intelligence" agencies. "RAND carries out traditional political, security, and economic research for these clients, as well as research on personnel issues, acquisition reform, and technical analyses." RAND's research includes investigation of political and economic trends to find the sources of potential regional conflict. RAND studies for these clients have included such titles as *Public Support for U.S. Military Operations, Can the Military Help Prevent Drug Use Among Youth?, Maximizing the Psychological Effects of Airpower: Lessons from Past Wars,* and *A Global Infrastructure to Support Expeditionary Aerospace Forces.*[216]

RAND also has key allied governments, prospective NATO partners and newly independent European states as clients, all with "strict adherence to its public interest charter and in consultation with the U.S. Department of Defense."[217]

Under an Air Force contract in the 1960s, RAND helped create the first computer network (and precursor to the Internet), ARPANET, intended to ensure the military would be able to maintain communications during a nuclear war. RAND's interest in the political and military uses of the Internet continues. For example, a recent RAND report explored *Employing Commercial Communications: Wideband Investment Options for the Department of Defense.* But RAND and others are also concerned about how citizens use the Internet. Wes Pedersen, communications director of the Public Affairs Council, warned that the Internet has become "the dream tool of activist groups that want to thwart the corporate power of multinationals," and declared that the Internet was a vehicle for "environmentalism, anti-free trade, anti-Americanism and, most astonishingly, anarchism." Pointing to NGO criticism of corporations like Nike, Monsanto and Shell, Pedersen claimed that "countering the growing influence of these cyber-powered anti-American, anti-corporate international organizations is one of the greatest challenges U.S. corporate and government PA practitioners will face in this new millennium."[218]

In an article originally published in *Comparative Strategy* in 1993, RAND researchers discussed the use of the Internet by activists promoting social change. A later RAND publication called *Zapatista Social Netwar in Mexico* examined the global Internet support the Zapatista movement enjoyed, and suggests ways that governments might respond to such activism.[219] The Defense Department's Special Operations and Low-Intensity Conflict office is further examining the dangers and uses of "netwar."[220]

TRANSATLANTIC BUSINESS DIALOGUE (TABD)

EU TABD OFFICE
115 RUE FROISSART
B-1040 BRUSSELS, BELGIUM
P 32 2 231 1728
WWW.TABD.COM

U.S. TABD OFFICE
1200 WILSON BLVD.
MC-RS-OO
ARLINGTON, VA 22209
P 703.465.3607
WWW.TABD.COM

The Transatlantic Business Dialogue was established in 1995 to be "a unique, business-driven process" for shaping European and U.S. policy on "barriers to business" and other trade issues.

"The TABD is an unprecedented venture in government-business partnership tackling issues relating to the world's most important economic relationship—that between the United States and the European Union. It has been called an 'experiment in entrepreneurial diplomacy' in which American and European business leaders at the CEO-level work together with a common objective of removing the remaining barriers to trade and investment. Their joint recommendations are communicated to senior-level U.S. and European Union officials who, in turn, work with business to develop effective policy with the ultimate goal of benefiting both economies through improved competitiveness and the creation of new jobs. The TABD has no formal structure and no official secretariat; nor is it a new institution or simply another business organization designed to influence policy makers. Rather, the TABD is a private-sector force designed to respond to the new reality of trade; namely that companies are now thinking and acting globally and their involvement in trade policy development is a natural outgrowth of such globalization."[221]

TABD's recommendations are presented at the biannual EU-US summits, and according to U.S. officials, most of them are adopted by the EU and U.S.[222] The tight relationship between TABD and government is no surprise, since TABD was established at the request of the European Commission and the U.S. Department of Commerce, which, in the words of then EU Commissioner Sir Leon Brittan, "asked businessmen from both sides of the Atlantic to get together and see if they could reach agreement on what needed to be done next. If they could, governments would be hard put to explain why it couldn't be done. The result was dramatic. European and American business leaders united in demanding more and faster trade liberalisation. And that had an immediate impact." At the EU Summit in June 1999, Brittan expressed satisfaction about the "clear, strong message of the usefulness of the TABD, and of the consensus between the Commission and industry on many important issues."[223]

The five TABD working groups deal with Standards and Regulatory Policy, Business Facilitation, Global Issues, Small and Medium Enterprises (SMEs) and E-Commerce. TABD makes recommendations on how to regulate (and deregulate) intellectual property rights, certification of the chemical and biotech industries and negotiations under the WTO. At the June 1999 annual conference U.S. President Clinton and German Chancellor Gerhard Schroeder called on the TABD to provide business input into the recovery plan for South Eastern Europe.[224] Journalists were barred from proceedings, even those involving EU commissioners and U.S. officials.

The TABD co-chairmen for 1999 were Konrad Eckenschwiller of the French employers organization MEDEF (Mouvement des Enterprises de France) and Xerox Vice President Mike Farren. The Chairmen for the year 2000 were George David (United Technologies) and Bertrand Collomb (LaFarge). Working groups are led by representatives from Xerox, Goodyear Tire, Siemens, Boeing, AT&T, Time Warner and other corporations.

A TABD CEO conference is held each year "to bring together business leaders and senior level government representatives to make constructive recommendations and measure progress on existing trade impediments. This unique combination of CEOs and senior government officials provides a unique opportunity to expand economic opportunities and to achieve breakthroughs on trade obstacles."

Globalisation is a positive-sum game—all sectors of society can benefit. Access to foreign markets allows more choice and better products, and allows economies to grow, increasing employment and access to higher education opportunities . . . However, the lack of success in launching a new trade round, and the demonstrations against the World Trade Organization (WTO) and other international institutions, reinforce the need to build confidence in global trade policy. Institutional reform will improve transparency and access to the multilateral process. The transatlantic business community is committed to promoting the positive benefits of the trade and working with governments to dispel the negative myths about trade liberalization. The TABD supports, as a first priority, the launch of an ambitious and broad-based round of trade negotiations as soon as possible...

TABD Mid Year Report May 23, 2000, Brussels, Belgium

TABD conferences have been in Seville, Spain in 1995, Chicago in 1996, Rome in 1997, Charlotte, North Carolina in 1998, and Berlin in 1999. The 2000 TABD meeting was held at the Omni Netherland Hotel in Cincinnati, Ohio on November 16-18. The conference brought "together more than 200 American and European CEOs and senior government officials to develop recommendations on how to best boost trade and investment. . . . Issues include the development of a common business agenda for future World Trade Organization (WTO) negotiations, the early accession of China to the WTO, the creation of industry-driven principles for e-commerce, and the utilization of an early warning system to resolve trade investment issues before they become disputes."[225]

TRILATERAL COMMISSION

NORTH AMERICAN GROUP
1156 FIFTEENTH STREET NW
WASHINGTON, DC 20005
P 202.467.5410

EUROPEAN GROUP
5, RUE DE TÉHÉRAN
75008 PARIS, FRANCE

PACIFIC ASIAN GROUP
4-9-17 MINAMI-AZABU
MINATO-KU, TOKYO 106, JAPAN
P 81.3.3446-7781
WWW.TRILATERAL.ORG

The Trilateral Commission was founded in 1973 by David Rockefeller, Zbigniew Brzezinski and others in order to foster cooperation between the U.S., Europe and Japan in shaping governmental and non-governmental action to renovate the international system after World War II. Recently focii have been globalization and labor markets, energy security, and "managing the international system."[226]

Members who take up positions in their national governments are supposed to give up their Trilateral Commission membership "to preserve the Commission's unofficial character."[227] Likewise, the consensus reached at Trilateral meetings is also informal and broad. As the Commission's website explains:

> "The Trilateral Commission does not adopt positions at its annual meetings agreed to by all participating members. The membership is too large and diverse for detailed agreement to be reached on a disputed issue. Differences are sometimes acute, resulting in unresolved debate. Members return home from the annual meeting with a variety of freshly informed perspectives on issues of concern with which they may or may not agree, but by which their own thinking is generally sharpened. The team of authors may reach detailed agreement on the issues addressed in particular task force reports. The Chairmen have sometimes issued statements at the conclusion of an annual meeting putting forward a few main themes and conclusions from the discussions."[228]

Membership currently includes about 335 businessmen, labor union leaders, academics, media executives and politicians from North America, Western Europe and Japan, led by three regional chairmen, currently:

• Paul Volcker (former Chairman of U.S. Federal Reserve Bank).
• Otto Graf Lambsdorff (German Minister of Economics, German

Bundestag 1972-98, Foundation Initiative of German Enterprises, Liberal International).

- Yotaro Kobayashi (Fuji Xerox, Nippon Telegraph and Telephone, Keizai Doyukai Japanese Association of Corporate Executive, Aspen Institute Japan, ABB Ltd.).

There is also an executive committee of 36, which currently includes executives from ABB, Mitsui, Mitsubishi, Levi Strauss and others.[229]

The annual meeting of Trilateral Commission members, typically three days long, rotates among the three regions: Vancouver in 1996, Tokyo in 1997, Berlin in 1998, Washington in 1999, and Tokyo in 2000. Roughly half of the members of the Trilateral Commission are likely to participate in any particular annual meeting. Each meeting also includes some participants from beyond the membership, including individuals from non-Trilateral countries.

"The program typically includes a few sessions devoted to current developments in each region, with special attention to the host country and region. Typically two sessions are framed by draft task force reports on particular issues, prepared by teams of authors from the three regions. Other sessions on key common issues are generally opened by a few panelists speaking from different perspectives. Luncheon and dinner sessions are often occasions for speeches by government leaders."[230]

The regional groups within the Trilateral Commission carry on some activities of their own. The European group, with its office in Paris, has an annual weekend meeting each fall. The North American group, with its office in New York, occasionally gathers with a special speaker for a dinner or luncheon event—as does the Japanese group, with its office in Tokyo.

Speakers at the 1999 annual meeting in Washington, DC were a who's who of power, including:

- Robert Zoellick (Center for Strategic and International Studies

---

Elected representatives agreed in the Uruguay Round to largely remove traditional tariffs as inefficient restraints on economic liberty. Consumers and their economies benefit directly through better access to high-quality goods, but many of these benefits can be thwarted by more insidious short-term, protectionist trade barriers. The new obstacles to trade are now domestic regulations. We draw attention to this fact—that liberalising efforts of our governments can be frustrated by routine, out-dated traditions and bureaucracy ... Non-tariff barriers to operations should be tackled with the same zeal. The TABD's ultimate objective is "approved once, accepted everywhere."

TABD Mid Year Report May 23, 2000, Brussels, Belgium

and former U.S. Undersecretary of State for Economic Affairs, now U.S. Trade Representative)
- Peter Sutherland (WTO/GATT, BP Amoco, Goldman Sachs, EC Commission)
- Lawrence Summers (then U.S. Deputy Secretary of the Treasury, now President of Harvard University)
- John Sweeney (AFL-CIO)
- John Manley (Canadian Minister of Industry)
- Javier Solana (Secretary-General of NATO)
- Lara Resende (formerly with National Development Bank of Brazil)
- Domingo Cavallo (former Economy Minister of Argentina)
- Andrei Kokoshin (former Russian First Minister of Defense)
- Serhiy Holovaty (Ukrainian Parliament)
- Rudolf Scharping (German Minister of Defense)
- John Deutch (MIT professor, former Director of U.S. Central Intelligence Agency)
- James Wolfensohn (President of World Bank)
- Stanley Fischer (International Monetary Fund)
- Toyoo Gyohten (Bank of Tokyo-Mitsubishi)
- Jim Leach (Chairman of U.S. House Banking and Financial Services Committee.

Programs and speeches from the past several meetings are available on the Trilateral Commission website.[231]

Funds for the Commission's initial meetings in the 1970s were provided by David Rockefeller, David Packard, George Franklin, the Kettering Foundation, the Ford Foundation, the Lilly Endowment, the Rockefeller Brothers Fund, the Thyssen Foundation, General Motors, Sears Roebuck, Caterpillar, Deere, Exxon, Texas Instruments, Coca Cola, Time, CBS, Wells Fargo Bank, Honeywell, Cargill, Cummins Engine, Kaiser Resources, Bechtel, Weyerhaeuser and others, and funding continues to come from corporations and corporate foundations.[232]

FOR MORE INFORMATION

Holly Sklar, editor, *Trilateralism: The Trilateral Commission and Elite Planning for World Management* (South End Press, 1980).

The TABD recognizes the efforts currently being undertaken to implement WTO rulings on the three outstanding transatlantic WTO cases (bananas, beef hormones and FSC).

TABD Mid Year Report May 23, 2000, Brussels, Belgium

UNION OF INDUSTRIAL AND EMPLOYERS' CONFEDERATIONS OF EUROPE (UNICE)

RUE JOSEPH II, 40 BTE 4
1000 BRUXELLES, BELGIUM
P 32.2.237.65.11
WWW.UNICE.ORG

UNICE was created in 1958 and now represents 34 business federations from 27 European countries (there is a list of them on the UNICE website). UNICE's mission is "to promote the common professional interests of the firms represented by its members; to inform the decision-making process at the European level so that policies and legislative proposals which affect business in Europe take account of companies' needs; and to represent its members in the dialogue between social partners enshrined in the Treaty on European Union."

UNICE's ten priorities are:[233]

- European competitiveness, a pre-condition for achieving healthy growth and a high-level of employment;
- Completion and implementation of the single market, to the benefit of 370 million consumers;
- Long-term stability of economic and monetary union with a sound single currency;
- A policy of open competition in the Union, offering greater choices and lower prices;
- Liberalisation of world trade by strengthening the multilateral trading system, based on fair and clear rules;
- Enlargement of the European Union to increase prosperity in the entire European continent;
- Better-quality legislation in order to minimise costs and constraints which are particularly harmful to the development of small and medium-sized enterprises;
- The promotion of entrepreneurship and the definition of social

policies based on economic realities and structural reforms
(lower taxation, more efficient public services, and more flexible
labour markets);

- Sustainable development through reconciling environmental
protection while stimulating the dynamism of European industry;
- Innovation and life-long learning—through targeted policies
for research, education and training, protection of intellectual
property, etc.—in order to meet the challenges of the information
and learning society.

There are UNICE working groups on:

- Economic and Financial Affairs (Competitiveness, Economic
and Monetary Union, Financial Services);
- External Relations (Customs Legislation, WTO, Trade and
Environment, Market Access, Export Credit Insurance);
- Industrial Affairs (Environment, Water, Waste, Air Quality,
Eco-Labeling, Transport, Energy, Telecommunications,
Technical Barriers to Trade);
- Social Affairs (Education and Training, Health and Safety at
Work, Industrial Relations, Labour Market);
- Company Affairs (Trade and Competition, State Aid, Cost Benefit
Analysis, International Business Practices, Environmental Liability,
Commercial and Judicial Law, Consumer/Marketing, Intellectual
Property Policy, Patents, Biotechnology).

UNICE Secretary-General Dirk Hudig was formerly a government rela-
tions executive with ICI (Imperial Chemical Industries). UNICE
President Georges Jacobs was formerly with the IMF and the Belgian
chemical and pharmaceutical corporation UCB. Former UNICE
President Francois Perigot was the head of Unilever France and AMUE
(Association for Monetary Union in Europe).

UNICE works with ERT, the EU Committee of the American

"While the ERT (The European Roundtable of Industrialists) subtly masterminds
its grand vision of Europe in collaboration with the European Commission, another
Brussels-based European lobby group is busy implementing the less glamorous
but equally critical details. Whereas ERT is quietly proactive, UNICE is a reactive,
detail-obsessed, supremely efficient lobby machine. Its working groups dissect
every proposal, regulation, directive and article emerging from Brussels before
spitting influential position papers back into the policy-making apparatus. Its efforts
often result in the adoption of business-friendly initiatives, and the blockage of more
socially or environmental progressive legislation."

in Belen Baleniga et al., Europe, Inc., 2000

Chamber of Commerce, the Transatlantic Business Dialogue and the major industry associations in Europe. UNICE's bias towards the biggest corporations resulted in a threat by the European Union for Artisans and Small and Medium-sized Enterprises (UEAPME) to sue UNICE in order to win a place in the European Union's Social Dialogue, which included UNICE and the major trade unions.

UNICE has a Brussels staff of forty, and a network of policy analysts divided into sixty working groups dealing with European business issues, including competitiveness, the Single Market and economic and monetary union. UNICE favors tax reductions for industry, reduced public spending on pensions, health and welfare, deregulation of trade and investment, enlargement of the European Union to include the 100 million consumers in eastern Europe and more subsidies for industrial infrastructure.

UNITED NATIONS

UN HEADQUARTERS
FIRST AVENUE AT 46TH STREET
NEW YORK, NY 10017
WWW.UN.ORG

The United Nations was created in 1945 by 51 founding nations as an international institution to maintain peace and security, solve economic and social problems and promote human rights.

The Security Council, which has veto power over the decisions of the UN General Assembly, is dominated by its five permanent members (the United States, Great Britain, France, Russia and China); ten additional members are elected by the General Assembly for two-year terms. Decisions on "substantive" matters require the concurring votes of all five permanent members, thus giving each of them veto power.

The UN has dozens of programs and agencies that provide forums for issues ranging from disaster relief and refugees, food, population, the environment, education, labor, trade and development, health, women and children. The International Court of Justice at the Hague (Netherlands) is the UN's official judicial organ.

The Security Council has made selective use of UN sanctions and "peace-keeping" forces in the Persian Gulf, Bosnian, and other conflicts, favoring corporate interests in the U.S. and Europe. In the 1990s, the U.S., led by Senator Jesse Helms, refused to pay its UN dues, further ensuring U.S. dominance (and the UN's impotence); the U.S. owes more than $1 billion. U.S. representatives to the UN have included such pro-business leaders as Henry Cabot Lodge, Jr. (1953-60), George W. Ball (1968), George Bush (1971-73), Andrew Young (1977-79), Jeane J. Kirkpatrick (1981-85), and Thomas Pickering (1989-92).

CORPORATE INFLUENCE OVER THE UN

In 1986, a draft UN Code of Conduct on Transnational Corporations called for corporations to comply with the laws of the countries within which they operated, and to refrain from lobbying their home country to influence the host nation's policies. Although the Code would not have been binding on corporations, corporations and the U.S. government pushed for further weakening of the Code, and in 1993, the UN's

Centre on Transnational Corporations (UNCTC) itself was dismantled. The UN Commission on Trade and Development (UNCTAD) was identified as the new UN department for work on corporations — but UNCTAD's focus is not to find ways to control corporations, but to stimulate corporate investment in the Third World.[234]

UNCTAD was established in 1964 to promote economic growth and development. In the 1980s, UNCTAD provided a forum for its member countries to negotiate international agreements on trade in commodities, which was folded into GATT. UNCTAD helps developing nations "take advantage" of liberalized trade under GATT and WTO, and administers a fund created to integrate developing nations into the world economy. Encouragement of corporate investment has become central to UNCTAD's work.

UNCTAD provided technical assistance to developing countries in connection with the GATT Uruguay Round of trade negotiations, helps developing countries find ways to "manage" their debts to the North and organized a Partners for Development summit meeting in November 1998 to facilitate cooperation between corporations, banks and development agencies. More than 2,700 representatives from 172 countries attended, and agreements were reached on public-private partnerships, investment promotion, agricultural commodities, sustainable development and biodiversity.[235]

The UN Development Program works "to achieve faster economic growth and better standards of living" by providing grants and technical assistance in 150 countries and working with forty international agencies. According to its 1994 executive board decision, sustainable development is the UNDP's guiding principle.[236]

The UN Development Program's 1999 *Human Development Report* (entitled *Globalization With a Human Face*) called for "tougher rules on global governance, including principles of performance for multinationals on labour standards, fair trade and environmental protection, [which] are needed to counter the negative effects of globalisation on the poorest nations," and called for the WTO to have "anti-monopoly functions over the activities of multinational corporations."[237] ICC Secretary-General Maria Cattaui responded by declaring that the UNDP was on 'the wrong track in calling for a mandatory code of conduct for multinationals.' Such binding rules, she argued, 'would put the clock back to a bygone era ... Governments in the poorer countries now compete to create a hospitable climate for foreign direct investment,' she concluded and referred to the ICC's cooperation with [UN Secretary-General Kofi] Annan and the UN as an example that 'times and perceptions have changed.'"[238]

Annan has declared that "people are poor not because of too much globalisation but too little," and has admitted that "a fundamental shift has occurred in recent years in the attitude of the United Nations towards the private sector. Confrontation has taken a back seat to cooperation. Polemics have given way to partnerships ... it is no surprise that the United Nations and the private sector are joining forces. The voice of business is now heard in United Nations policy debates."[239]

In July 2000, a "Global Compact" was announced by Annan after meeting with a delegation from the International Chamber of Commerce (ICC), including representatives from the energy corporation Norsk Hydro, mining giant Rio Tinto, consumer products leader Unilever, Shell, industrial and military electronics contractor Siemens and other major corporations.

"Annan described this new international covenant between the UN and business as 'the most sensible way forward to safeguard open markets while at the same time creating a human face for the global economy.' Despite the flawed social and environmental records of involved corporations including Rio Tinto, Siemens and Norsk Hydro, this agreement on 'global corporate citizenship' is completely non-binding, with no enforcement mechanisms whatsoever. At a time when global economic deregulation has made mandatory and enforceable international rules for corporate behaviour more necessary than ever, the Global Compact is a questionable initiative."[240]

The Global Compact was first proposed by Annan at the January 1999 World Economic Forum in Davos, because of his "fear that, if we do not act, there may be a threat to the open global market, and especially to the multilateral trade regime."[241] In a June 1998 speech to the U.S. Chamber of Commerce Annan had warned that:

> As you know, globalisation is under intense pressure. And business is in the line of fire, seen by many as not doing enough in the areas of environment, labour standards and human rights. This may not seem fair, but it is a perception that will not go away unless business is seen to be committed to global corporate citizenship. The Global Compact offers a reasonable way out of this impasse.[242]

In their joint statement announcing the Global Compact, the UN and the ICC called for a new round of international trade negotiations because it would "contribute to reinforcing the economic momentum generated by trade liberalisation"—precisely the reason 1,200 groups from around the world had called for a comprehensive review of existing trade agreements before any new negotiations were undertaken.

Implementation of the Global Compact is to be facilitated by the

UN Secretary-General, the International Labour Organisation, the UN Environment Programme and the UN High Commissioner for Human Rights. Journalists reported that "privately, UN officials admit that they will not be able to check if companies do respect the voluntary agreement on good practice," and that "[n]either UN officials nor private sector leaders were able to say how their new-found cooperation would translate into practice when dealing with multinationals accused of degrading the environment or working with governments violating human or labour rights."[243]

U.S. CHAMBER OF COMMERCE

1615 H STREET NW
WASHINGTON, DC 20062
P 202.659.6000
WWW.USCHAMBER.ORG

Often called the largest business association in the world, the Chamber of Commerce claims to represent three million companies, 3,000 state and local chambers of commerce, 830 business associations, and 87 American Chambers of Commerce in over 40 countries.[244]

Local chambers of commerce were being established in the United States before 1800, and many of them joined the United States Chamber of Commerce when it was created in 1912. The U.S. Chamber was established (at the suggestion of President Taft) to support uniform business and trade policies and standards. In the post-World War II era the Chamber was not very active politically, instead sponsoring workshops on the evils of Communism.[245] However, the Chamber was revitalized in the 1970s as its membership and budget grew several-fold and it relocated to Washington, DC. By 1980, the Chamber's budget was $55 million and it had 45 full-time lobbyists.

The Chamber donates a substantial portion of its current $70 million budget to politicians. The Chamber's political action committee (PAC) donated more than $10 million to federal candidates in 1997-98, 90 percent of it to Republicans,[246] and spent another $17 million on lobbying in 1998.[247]

The Chamber's structure includes policy committees, councils, task forces and a staff of 1,200 governed by a 100-member board of directors.[248]

The Chamber has Councils devoted to Small Business, Employee Benefits, Environment and Energy, Food and Agriculture, International Policy, Labor Relations, Regulatory Affairs, Taxation, Technology Policy, Transportation Infrastructure and other issues.

Task forces deal with Antitrust, Electricity Deregulation, Export Finance, Foreign Commercial Relations, Global Telecommunications, Privatization, Social Security, Water Works and the World Trade Organization.

The Chamber has a National Chamber Litigation Center to take legal action against environmental, workplace and consumer regulations,[249] and an Institute for Legal Reform to attack the ability of agencies and citizens to hold corporations accountable in courts of law. As the Chamber's website says:

> When persuasion, lobbying and negotiation fail, American business has one more recourse—the U.S. Chamber's law firm, the National Chamber Litigation Center (NCLC). The Institute for Legal Reform, an affiliate of the U.S. Chamber, is leading the fight against a handful of lawyers who are sucking the vitality out of American business through a wave of frivolous class action lawsuits.[250]

Since 1977, the Litigation Center (a tax-exempt affiliate and legal arm of the Chamber) has participated in nearly 600 lawsuits.

The Institute for Legal Reform, also tax-exempt, was created in 1998 "to reduce excessive and frivolous litigation while restoring fairness and balance to the nation's civil justice system. First tobacco. Then guns, followed by lead paint. What industry will be the next target of lawsuits?" The Institute supports legislation such as the Litigation Fairness Act (S. 1269/H.R. 2597), which would prevent the government from filing lawsuits against corporations, as it has in the case of the tobacco, gun and lead paint industries, and the Interstate Class Action Jurisdiction Act (H.R. 1875/ S. 353), which would require more class action lawsuits against corporations to be heard in federal court rather than in State courts.

The Chamber website claims that 96 percent of its members are businesses with less than 100 employees. "No company is too small—or too big—to be a U.S. Chamber member. That's because U.S. Chamber members share a common goal: our fight for free enterprise." The Chamber then lists the kinds of members it has, as if they were equal in stature and power: "The neighborhood dry cleaner. The state chamber of commerce. A Fortune 500 company. A trade association. Home based-business."[251]

While the Chamber does have grassroots support, its policies tend to mirror the positions of its largest corporate members. Other organizations, including the conservative National Federation of Independent

---

We haven't done anything for business this week—but it is only Monday morning.

President Lyndon Johnson,
speech to U.S. Chamber of Commerce,
April 27, 1964

Business (NFIB), accuse the Chamber of being too big-business oriented.[252] In 1983, when even Ronald Reagan realized tax increases were inevitable, the White House lobbied 12,000 state and local chambers of commerce, asking them to ignore the U.S. Chamber's calls to reject all tax increases.[253]

The Chamber seeks to reduce taxes and welfare payments (called welfare "reform"), to limit the liability of corporations that are sued (called "tort reform"), and to influence workplace issues such as labor organizing, pensions and health care benefits, and pushes for free trade.

The Chamber's TradeRoots program's motto is "Growing Prosperity in America and the World." TradeRoots works to build a "winning trade coalition in the U.S. Congress and stop the anti-trade protectionism." To do this, TradeRoots aims to: "Shore up and sustain pro-trade coalitions at the grassroots level in 66 congressional districts in 27 states to work for swift passage of China PNTR and other vital trade initiatives; Identify and mobilize community leaders as pro-trade advocates in each district; Partner with the governor of each state to communicate the local benefits of trade; Tell our success stories through local media, using a vigorous communications campaign; and, Establish a one-stop information resource on trade—on the web and off the web—for everything from state and local trade statistics to success stories."[254] TradeRoots and the U.S. Department of Commerce are co-sponsoring a two-day program to "give chamber executives the tools needed to make their members global business leaders."

The National Chamber Foundation was created in the 1960s to fund research and promote a favorable image of business in the public eye. The Foundation now co-sponsors an annual "economic summit" in Washington, DC with the World Economic Forum *(see profile of WEF on page 137)*; the WEF-NCF meeting in May 2000 was attended by 300 participants from more than 40 nations.[255]

"If you go to (a regulatory) agency first, don't be too pessimistic if they can't solve your problem there. If they don't, that's what the task force is for. Two weeks ago (a group) showed up and I asked if they had a problem. They said they did, and we made a couple phone calls and straightened it out, alerted the top people at the agency that there was a little hanky-panky going on at the bottom of the agency, and it was cleared up very rapidly—so the system does work if you use it as a sort of an appeal. We can act as a double check on the agency that you might encounter problems with."

C. Boyden Gray (counsel to the U.S. President Ronald Reagan's Task Force on Regulatory Relief), in a speech to the Chamber of Commerce in the early 1980s (quoted in David Vogel, Fluctuating Fortunes, *1989)*

In 1999, the Chamber of Commerce hosted a "Brownfields to American Dream Fields" conference to facilitate the "revitalization" of brownfields (abandoned—and often toxic—manufacturing sites) into recreational facilities. A highlight of the event was the "Let's Make a Deal session, where cities presented their available brownfield sites to developers, the financial community, and government agencies." In June 2000, the Chamber and AIG Environmental (an insurance corporation) hosted a follow-up conference entitled "Let's Make It Happen" to promote "creative public and private partnerships."[256] These "partnerships" often are deals wherein the public buys and cleans up the toxic sites abandoned by corporations.

Public-private partnerships are so important that the Chamber has established a Center for Corporate Citizenship (CCC) to facilitate them. The CCC "fosters corporate citizenship by celebrating corporate achievements, developing and sharing public policy recommendations, documenting and publicizing corporate best practices, and facilitating public-private sector partnerships." Sponsors include Texaco, Cargill, Conoco, General Motors, Lockheed Martin, Mitsubishi Motors America, State Farm Insurance, Unocal, the American Apparel Manufacturers Association, the Prince of Wales Business Leaders Forum, and the U.S. Council for International Business—clearly businesses that are in great need of subsidies in the form of public-private partnerships. In September 2000, the CCC held a conference on Corporate Citizenship and the Future of Private-Public Cooperation to "find out how to improve the climate for public-private cooperation, manage the contributions and expectations of partners, and identify opportunities for collaboration between business, government and non-profits." This was followed in October by the "First Annual Military Community Summit" to be followed by a "gala event" sponsored by the CCC.[257]

The Center for International Private Enterprise (CIPE) is an affiliate of the U.S. Chamber of Commerce that receives funding from at least two U.S. government agencies (the U.S. Agency for International Development and the U.S. Information Agency) as well as from private organizations, such as the National Endowment for Democracy. CIPE promotes economic "reform," private enterprise and "democratic consolidation" around the world. CIPE "aggressively spreads a pro-business, pro-freedom message and administers programs to train future leaders in emerging democracies around the world."[258]

U.S. EXPORT-IMPORT BANK

811 VERMONT AVE NW
WASHINGTON DC 20571
P 800.565.3946
WWW.EXIM.GOV

The ExIm Bank is the official export credit agency of the United States. It was created in 1934 in order to stimulate exports from the United States. The ExIm (1) provides guarantees of working capital loans for U.S. exporters, (2) guarantees the repayment of loans or makes loans to foreign purchasers of U.S. goods and services, and (3) provides credit insurance against non-payment by foreign buyers for political or commercial risk. Following are a few examples of ExIm projects:[259]

- ExIm is backing a $77 million loan from Citicorp to Bulgaria so that Westinghouse can modernize the Kozloduy nuclear power plant.
- In August 2000, the ExIm Bank signed a Project Incentive Agreement with the Nigerian government and the Central Bank of Nigeria to increase U.S. exports for Nigerian private sector infrastructure projects. The ExIm Bank has similar agreements with Vietnam, Russia, Turkmenistan, Georgia, Armenia and Ukraine.
- ExIm is financing the $36 million export of Motorola telecommunications equipment to the Dominican Republic.
- ExIm is providing $490 million in loan guarantees for Tyumen Oil of Russia to buy oil refinery equipment and engineering services from ABB Lummus Global, Halliburton and other suppliers, for the Ryazan oil refinery near Moscow and the Samotlor oil field in western Siberia.

The top ten corporate recipients of ExIm Bank financing in 1998 included aerospace giant Boeing ($2.6 billion), earthmoving equipment and engine manufacturer Caterpillar ($390 million), Westinghouse ($197), the petrochemical services corporation Halliburton ($150 million), and General Motors ($138 million)—as well as the Japanese corporation Marubeni ($186 million) and the Swiss engineering corporation ABB Asea Brown Boveri ($215 million). Boeing was the top recipient in 1996, 1997 and 1998.[260]

Amidst charges of bribery, and after personal lobbying by U.S. President Clinton, Brazil awarded a $1.4 billion contract to the U.S. military contractor Raytheon. The contract calls for Raytheon to construct SIVAM, a high-tech radar, surveillance and weapon systems covering 22 million square kilometers of the Amazon. The ostensible purpose of SIVAM is to map soil, terrain, minerals and vegetation, expose drug smugglers, support air traffic control and climatological studies and strengthen border security and communications. Critics fear the system will also be used to survey and sell timber, minerals, and oil and gas, and point to Mitsubishi, Lockheed and other corporations that have purchased aerial photographs of the Amazon from E-Systems, a Raytheon contractor, to prospect for oil, timber, and minerals. More than $1 billion of the financing will come from the U.S. ExIm Bank, on the grounds that the construction of the system will employ many Americans.[261]

ExIm was involved in a $1.3 billion loan for the sale of Sikorsky helicopters to Turkey, and Sikorsky, a subsidiary of United Technologies, is likely to make another $360 million by exporting thirty helicopters as part of the recent $1.3 billion package of U.S. military aid to Colombia. Sikorsky is represented by Congressman Sam Gejdenson, the ranking member of the U.S. House International Relations Committee, and by Christopher Dodd, ranking member of the U.S. Senate Foreign Relations Subcommittee on Narcotics. Former U.S. Representative Gerald Solomon (R-NY), a lobbyist for the Colombia aid package, said the support of Dodd and Gejdenson was "absolutely crucial." Dodd and Gejdenson opposed military intervention in Latin America during the 1980s, but recently changed their minds. Between 1997 and early 2000, Gejdenson received $19,000 in political contributions from United Technologies and Dodd received $33,200. The Texas Congressional delegation helped secure the sale of 33 Huey helicopters manufactured by Bell Helicopter Textron, which hired lobbyist Tony Gillespie, a former U.S. ambassador to Colombia. "It's business for us, and we are as aggressive as anybody," said a Bell lobbyist. "I'm just trying to sell helicopters."[262]

Loans for weapons exports, which might be opposed by Congress if they were to come from the Pentagon, are sometimes arranged through the ExIm Bank's "dual use" program under which aircraft and equipment that can be used for both military and civilian purposes, such as the recent $44 million in ExIm loans to Indonesia for spare parts for military aircraft, and a $90 million loan to Romania to finance the purchase of five Lockheed Martin radar systems. "Because transport and communications projects that fit ExIm's 'dual use' definition will be an important part of NATO expansion, ExIm loans are likely to be utilized as yet another important avenue for subsidizing the growth of the alliance."[263]

The ExIm is a government-held corporation governed by a board of directors consisting of: James A. Harmon (Schroder Wertheim international investment bank), Jackie M. Clegg (staff to U.S. Senator Jake Garn and Senate committees), Dan Renberg (staff for U.S. Senator Arlen Specter, attorney for Wiley, Rein & Fielding), Dorian Vanessa Weaver (White House staff for U.S. President Clinton, Engineering Research Associates), U.S. Secretary of Commerce William M. Daley (son of Chicago mayor, attorney with Mayer, Brown & Platt, President of Amalgamated Bank of Chicago), and U.S. Trade Representative Charlene Barshefsky (trade attorney with Steptoe & Johnson).

U.S. FEDERAL RESERVE BANK

20TH STREET AND
CONSTITUTION AVE NW
WASHINGTON DC 20551
P 202.452.3000
WWW.FEDERALRESERVE.GOV

The Federal Reserve, the central bank of the United States, was founded by Congress in 1913 "to provide the nation with a safer, more flexible, and more stable monetary and financial system." The Federal Reserve Bank describes itself as a government agency, and its duties as (1) conducting the nation's monetary policy; (2) supervising and regulating banking institutions and protecting the credit rights of consumers; (3) maintaining the stability of the financial system; and (4) providing certain financial services to the U.S. government, the public, financial institutions and foreign official institutions. As discussed in Part 1, central banks are actually quasi-official corporations with unique and enormous power to set interest rates, loan money to banks and to the government itself, and to transfer currency and gold to and from other countries.

There are twelve regional Federal Reserve Banks, in Boston, New York, Philadelphia, Cleveland, Richmond, Atlanta, Chicago, St. Louis, Minneapolis, Kansas City, Dallas and San Francisco.

The Federal Reserve's board of governors consists of seven bankers appointed by the U.S. President and confirmed by the U.S. Senate to serve 14-year terms of office. Members may serve only one term. The President also designates, with Senate confirmation, two members of the board to be chairman and vice chairman, for four-year terms.[264]

The seven board members constitute a majority of the twelve-member Federal Open Market Committee (FOMC), which makes decisions affecting the cost and availability of money and credit in the economy. The other five members of the FOMC are Reserve Bank presidents, one of whom is the president of the Federal Reserve Bank of New York.[265]

The members of the board "routinely confer with officials of other government agencies, representatives of banking industry groups, officials of the central banks of other countries, members of Congress and academicians. For example, they meet frequently with Treasury officials and the Council of Economic Advisers to help evaluate the economic climate and to discuss objectives for the nation's economy. Governors also discuss the international monetary system with central bankers of other countries and are in close contact with the heads of the U.S. agencies that make foreign loans and conduct foreign financial transactions."[266]

Alan Greenspan, current chairman of the Federal Reserve, was originally appointed in 1987 by U.S. President Reagan. Under his leadership, the Fed bailed out Long-Term Capital Management, a hedge fund with several former Fed officials on its board, and cut interest rates three times to prop up weak Asian and Latin American currencies and the Dow Jones.[267]

U.S. OVERSEAS PRIVATE INVESTMENT CORPORATION
(OPIC)

1100 NEW YORK AVE NW
WASHINGTON, DC 20527
P 202.336.8595
WWW.OPIC.GOV

The mission of the Overseas Private Investment Corporation (OPIC), part of the U.S. Department of State, is "to mobilize and facilitate the participation of United States private capital and skills in the economic and social development of less developed countries and areas, and countries in transition from nonmarket to market economies, thereby complementing the development assistance objectives of the United States."

OPIC accomplishes this mission by providing loans, guarantees and insurance to U.S. corporations operating overseas. OPIC insures investments against three different risks:

- *Inconvertibility of currency,* which protects investors from increased restrictions on the investor's ability to "convert local currency into U.S. dollars" (in other words, remove their profits from the host country).
- *Expropriation coverage* provides compensation for losses due to confiscation, nationalization, or governmental actions that "deprive the investor of its fundamental rights in the investment."
- *Political risk insurance,* which covers investors against losses caused by "politically motivated acts of violence [such as] war, revolution, insurrection or civil strife, including terrorism and sabotage."[268]

OPIC's rationale is that "private sector investment overseas contributes substantially to both the national and foreign policy interests of U.S. citizens. It strengthens and expands the U.S. economy by improving U.S. competitiveness in the international marketplace. It also helps less developed nations expand their economies and become valuable markets for U.S. goods and services, thereby increasing U.S. exports and creating U.S. jobs."

OPIC also "advocates on behalf of U.S. business clients that have made long-term investments in emerging markets and developing nations.

OPIC

OPIC also works with host country governments to help create economic climates that attract U.S. investment, facilitating the entry of hundreds of U.S. businesses into new markets abroad."[269]

OPIC also sponsors seminars and conferences and works with other federal government agencies, state and local governments, private organizations and multilateral institutions to "increase awareness" among U.S. companies of the "real opportunities for business expansion through overseas investment."

OPIC claims to have supported (corporate) investments worth nearly $130 billion in 140 countries, generated $61 billion in U.S. (corporate) exports, and helped to create 242,000 American jobs. OPIC-backed projects include agribusiness, telecommunications, financial services, manufacturing, mining, energy and transportation. Like many other national and multinational agencies, OPIC is also using government-guaranteed subsidies to support "privatization" projects.[270]

OPIC is typically financing and insuring 400 corporations. Its project lists are published as part of its annual report, and they are available in the OPIC website. Below is a table of recent projects.

OPIC complements the entry of U.S. government agencies and corporations into new markets such as Eastern Europe *(see the profile of NATO on page 93)*. In early 2000, OPIC and the U.S. Trade Development Agency (TDA) opened an office in Croatia to promote U.S. (corporate) investment in Southeast Europe, following trips by U.S. Secretary of State Madeleine Albright.[271]

OPIC's $350 million New Africa Infrastructure Fund for investment in the sub-Sahara is expected to leverage an additional $2 billion of corporate investment which will generate $50 million in annual revenues for African countries — and $350 million in American exports.[272]

OPIC's focus on promoting investment is understandable in the light of its unique role in providing insurance against political risk. As OPIC points out, all of its guaranty and insurance obligations "are backed by the full faith and credit of the United States of America," and the threat of U.S. government intervention is usually enough. Of the more than 6,700 contracts that OPIC and its predecessor agency

---

The existence of OPIC's expropriation insurance is undoubtedly a deterrent to nationalization without compensation. (G)overnments have failed to follow through on announced plans to nationalize OPIC-insured investment because we were able to bring to the attention of the governments concerned the fact of OPIC's involvement . . . Unfortunately, we are unable to discuss these particular cases publicly.

OPIC's general counsel Marshall Mays (as quoted in
U.S. Congressional Research Service, September 4, 1973)

(the U.S. Agency for International Development) have issued since 1966, only 263 resulted in insurance claims—resulting in $545 million in payments to investors. Three-fourths of the claims were related to expropriation; twenty percent were for incontrovertibility; five percent to civil strife, and less than 1 percent to war damage. More than two-thirds of the claims were to corporations operating in Latin America, and have included reimbursing U.S. mining corporations such as Kennecott and Anaconda.[273]

Recipient	Location	Project
Citibank	Central America and Caribbean	Central American and Caribbean Investment Facility, a $200 million medium-to-long-term lending facility to support private sector development (February 1999)
Entergy Power Group	Bulgaria	Privitization and modernization of the 840-megawatt lignate-fired Maritza East III power plant.[274]
Soros Private Fund Management (SPFM)	Albania, Bulgaria, Bosnia, Herzegovina, Croatia, Macedonia, Romania, Slovenia, Turkey, and Montenegro, "an emerging consumer market of 112 million people."	$100 million loan guaranty for the Southwest Europe Equity Fund managed by SPFM, which wil be required to raise $50 million of equity capital. OPIC already provides $65 million in financing and insurance for projects in Bulgaria, Croatia and Romania, and other OPIC-supported funds have invested more than $30 million in the region.[275]
Atlantic Methanol Production Co. (CMS Enterprises and Nobel Affiliates and the Guinean government)	Equatorial Guinea	$173 million guaranty and up to $200 million in political risk insurance for a $450 million methanol plant on the island of Bioko.[276]
Ritz-Carlton Hotel Company	Turkey	$50 million loan guaranty to build a $222 million hotel and convention facility.[277]
Enron Corporation	Guatemala	$50 million in financing for the expansion of an electric power generation facility that will supply 20 percent of Guatemala's electricity.[278]
InterOil Limited	Papua New Guinea	Loan guaranty up to $85 million for the construction and operation of an oil refinery and storage facility near Port Moresby.[279]

USA*ENGAGE

1300 CONNECTICUT AVE NW
WASHINGTON, DC 20036
P 202.822.9491
WWW.USAENGAGE.ORG

The telephone number listed for USA*Engage is actually for the Fratelli Group public relations firm.

USA*Engage, created in April 1997, is a coalition of 674 corporations and industry associations. USA*Engage states that "economic strength is integral to our nation's security and worldwide leadership," and promotes deregulated international trade because "the ability of American farmers, workers and businesses to compete in emerging markets is central to our own economic prosperity and to the worldwide growth of democracy, freedom, and human rights."[280]

USA*Engage members include Exxon, Boeing, General Motors, Georgia-Pacific, the Business Roundtable, the National Association of Manufacturers, the National Cattlemen's Beef Association, the U.S. Chamber of Commerce, U.S.-China Business Council, and the U.S. Council for International Business and Trade, the American Farm Bureau Federation, Chase Manhattan Bank and the Chemical Manufacturers Association.[281]

Richard Albrecht, senior advisor to the Boeing Company and a representative of USA*Engage, testified before a U.S. House Subcommittee on International Trade Committee that the group was "founded by the leaders of the National Foreign Trade Council . . . to give a voice to the concerns we in the international business, trade, and humanitarian aid community have about the current [trade] sanctions process."

The mixed motivations are apparent in his testimony that "today two-thirds of all Boeing airplanes produced are shipped overseas. We must have continued access to foreign markets, especially those emerging economies with fledgling airlines because their initial purchases usually establish what brand they will buy in the long-run. Unilateral sanctions are unpredictable, and for our business that spells trouble. . . . Today [Boeing is] precluded from selling aircraft in seven countries, and at least eleven more markets are at risk because of current or potential [U.S. trade] sanctions. We estimate the market potential in these at-risk countries to be about $175 billion during the next twenty years. What we need is a process that will give our businesses, humanitarian organizations, and NGOs some assurance their investments in a country will not be wiped out indiscriminately by a unilateral sanction." Albrecht went on to complain that trade sanctions also blocked the public financing subsidies upon which U.S. exporters rely—and then claimed that "the only losers will be the American worker."[282]

USA*Engage Vice Chairman Frank Kittredge testified before the U.S. Congress that because of U.S. trade sanctions imposed after China's 1989 Tiananmen Square crackdown, U.S. corporations had not been allowed to bid on more than $15 billion worth of nuclear power business in China. "Beyond losing this significant business opportunity and the thousands of U.S. jobs associated with it, the award to non-U.S. suppliers had the effect of completely isolating the U.S. from the Chinese nuclear energy program, which has progressed very well without U.S. involvement."[283]

USA*Engage Chairman William C. Lane (who is also the Washington director for governmental affairs of Caterpillar Inc.), testifying before the Senate Task Force on Economic Sanctions on behalf of both USA*Engage and Caterpillar, complained that U.S. sanctions in the early 1980s allowed Caterpillar's Japanese competitor Komatsu to capture Soviet pipeline work.[284]

While USA*Engage opposes continuing sanctions against Cuba,[285] it also opposes sanctions based on human rights violations. For example, USA*Engage challenged a Massachusetts state law giving preferential treatment to companies that do not do business with Burma's military dictatorship. The European Union and Japan challenged the state law on the grounds that it violated the World Trade Organization rules that forbid the consideration of non-commercial factors such as

---

Mother Jones calls USA*Engage a strategic "front" organization of Boeing and other Fortune 500 corporations seeking to put a positive spin on business with dictatorial regimes. In one example, the magazine cites internal USA*Engage memos stating, Boeing will contact Rev. Billy Graham "to enlist his support against the so-called Religious Persecution Act before Congress, which will limit U.S. trade with nations that suppress religious freedom. Although 60 other evangelical leaders last week urged President Clinton to support the pro-religion bill, Graham has come out against it. He argues trade restrictions harm rather than help international relations—which is Boeing's position. Graham has also actively supported Boeing's effort to maintain China's most-favored-nation trade, despite its history of human-rights violations.

Rick Anderson, Seattle Weekly, *May 7, 1998*

human rights in government procurement policies, and require that all countries be treated the same, regardless of their conduct. Meanwhile, USA*Engage challenged the Massachusetts law as a violation of the U.S. Constitutional principal that the U.S. President alone has the authority to conduct foreign policy. Both the Massachusetts and U.S. courts agreed with USA*Engage, and the WTO panel also ruled against Massachusetts.[286]

In a June 2000 press release, the National Foreign Trade Council and USA*Engage "hailed today's unanimous U.S. Supreme Court decision to strike down the Massachusetts 'Burma Law' as a victory for the U.S. Constitution.... We are very pleased with the Supreme Court's decision, which reaffirms the federal government's predominant role in foreign policy and should help put an end to state and local efforts to make foreign policy." NFTC filed the suit "because of concerns among U.S. businesses and agriculture that the mounting patchwork of state and local sanctions was threatening to seriously hurt U.S. interests" and threatened a coherent U.S. foreign policy.[287] As always, corporate power prefers a centralized political system and opposes having to deal with communities and local governments, and equates corporate interests with U.S. interests.

To underscore the bipartisan nature of corporate power, the lawsuit against Massachusetts had the support of former U.S. government officials like President Gerald Ford, national security advisors Brent Scowcroft and Frank C. Carlucci and Defense Secretaries Richard Cheney and Alexander Haig, Defense Secretary and World Bank President Robert S. McNamara, Edwin Meese, III, G. William Miller, the U.S. Chamber of Commerce, the National Association of Manufacturers, the American Petroleum Institute, the American Farm Bureau Federation, the Chemical Manufacturers Association and the Solicitor General of the United States.[288]

USA*Engage tracks existing and proposed sanctions at the U.S. state and local levels.[289]

In December 1999, USA*Engage expressed its disappointment that the WTO Ministerial in Seattle had failed to secure a new round of multilateral trade negotiations, but eight months later found reasons to praise the free trade platforms of the Democratic and Republican National Parties.[290]

USA*Engage has an "International Trade Mall" webpage[291] that includes links to:

- federal government agencies that provide subsidies and marketing for U.S. exporters, including the U.S. State Department, the

U.S. Export-Import Bank, the U.S. Department of Commerce's International Trade Administration, and the U.S. International Trade Commission;

- U.S. Congressional committees with jurisdiction over trade, healthcare, Social Security, welfare, transportation, communications, consumer affairs, national security, foreign policy and international economic policy;
- the Virtual Trade Mission Group of corporate leaders from the U.S. President's Export Council, which propagandizes "middle school, high school and college students as part of a new communications strategy for the PEC to increase public awareness of the importance of America's export economy and the need to form a bi-partisan public-private strategy to meet the challenges of the global marketplace."
- multilateral organizations such as the Organization for Economic Cooperation and Development (OECD), the Trade and Development Centre (a joint venture of the World Bank and the World Trade Organization), and the European Union;
- pro-business think tanks and advocacy organizations, including the American Enterprise Institute, the Brookings Institution, the Cato Institute, Citizens for a Sound Economy, the Council on Foreign Relations, the European-American Business Council and the Heritage Foundation.

WORLD BANK/ INTERNATIONAL MONETARY FUND

WORLD BANK
1818 H STREET NW
WASHINGTON DC 20433
WWW.WORLDBANK.ORG
P 202.473.1000

INTERNATIONAL
MONETARY FUND (IMF)
700 19TH STREET NW
WASHINGTON DC 20431
P 202.623.7300
WWW.IMF.ORG

The World Bank (the International Bank for Reconstruction and Development) and International Monetary Fund were established at the end of World War II under agreements reached (by the victors) at the United Nations Monetary and Financial Conference held at Bretton Woods, New Hampshire. The institutional blueprints closely resembled plans proposed by task forces led by the Council on Foreign Relations and the U.S. government.

The World Bank provides loans and gives commercial and investment banks incentives for investing in developing countries. The related International Monetary Fund (IMF) was created to promote international monetary cooperation, to facilitate the expansion of international trade, and to provide temporary financial assistance to debtor countries. A third institution, which would negotiate international trade rules, was envisioned but not created because of concerns about the loss of national sovereignty. Fifty years later, the World Trade Organization was finally created, and fears of loss of sovereignty are being fulfilled (*see profile of World Trade Organization on page 139*).

The ostensible purposes of the World Bank and IMF were to reconstruct after the war, and to prevent the return of the trade barriers, unstable exchange rates, and inflation that had contributed to the war. The actual effects have been to force open the world's local economies to multinational corporations. So much of the Bank's loans go to oil, gas and mining projects that it has been called the "largest single purveyor of the 'development' model that has razed the social and ecological foundations of the nonindustrial world."[292]

An "essential aspect" of the IMF's responsibilities is surveillance: overseeing the economic and social policies of the nations that receive

financial aid, making sure debtors are "complying with their obligations . . . in order to ensure the effective operation of the international
monetary system."[293] The IMF's financial aid is usually tied to the
requirement that the debtor undergo structural adjustments, including
privatization (selling public agencies and resources to corporations),
exporting resources and goods at the expense of local subsistence,
raising interest rates and lowering wages, providing open markets and
subsidies to foreign corporations and, eventually, to even more debt.
As discussed earlier, most of the countries that have undergone structural adjustment programs (SAPs) are worse off than they were before-
hand. And much of the IMF "aid" to nations that cannot keep up their
debt payments actually bails out Northern banks and stockholders from
their speculative investments *(see section on structural adjustment programs in Part 1)*.

World Bank loans and insurance encourage commercial banks to
invest in ill-advised projects they would otherwise shun. The World
Bank enriches corporations in other ways as well. A bit over half of the
$25 billion loaned by the World Bank each year is disbursed in the coun-
try where the project takes place. The other half is disbursed directly
to the corporations that are contracted to carry out World Bank projects. Corporations hire former World Bank staff as lobbyists to help
them win the contracts. Contracts with consultants, which cost ten percent of the World Bank's $25 billion, are not even competitively bid.[294]

The World Bank has set up an Internet-based marketing and
information service called PrivatizationLink, which advertises "investment opportunities arising from privatization in developing countries
and transition economies."[295] The program's initial focus is selling off
public agencies and resources in Eastern Europe, Central Asia, and
Subsaharan Africa, but public property and agencies are being sold off
everywhere. More than 10,000 public companies were privatized
between 1988 and 1998, and no wonder: privatization is part of 70
percent of the IMF's structural adjustment program (SAP) loans, and
40 percent of the World Bank's sectoral adjustment loans. Public property is commonly sold at a fraction of its value, often without any
competitive bidding, and often without any regulatory system to prevent the stripping and exporting of the assets. A former chief economist for the World Bank has admitted that it "has proved difficult to
prevent corruption and other problems" and that the "advocates of
privatization may have overestimated the benefits . . . and underesti-
mated the costs, particularly the political costs . . ."[296]

The World Bank and IMF consist of member nations but are controlled by the governmental and corporate financial leaders of the U.S., Europe, and Japan.[297]

World Bank Group is composed of the International Finance Corporation (IFC), the International Bank for Reconstruction and Development (IBRD), the International Development Association (IDA), and the Multilateral Guarantee Agency (MIGA).

International Finance Corporation (IFC) was created in 1956 to "encourage private sector activity in developing countries." The IFC finances private sector (corporate) projects and helps companies in developing nations borrow money from the international capital markets. "Working in partnership with major international investment and commercial banks, IFC structures, underwrites, and distributes the clients' securities. Securities are placed exclusively with major international institutional investors to ensure that securities are held by stable, long-term portfolio investors." In other words, the IFC helps companies in the South go into debt to the major banks in the North. Since its founding, IFC has committed more than $26 billion of its own funds and has arranged $18 billion in syndications and underwriting for 2,264 companies in 135 developing countries.[298]

International Bank for Reconstruction and Development (IBRD) is the World Bank itself, which provides loans and development assistance to middle-income countries and creditworthy poorer countries (as opposed to the World Bank Group's IDA *(see below)*. The money for IBRD loans comes from the sale of World Bank bonds to investment managers, bank trusts, insurance companies and pension funds. For example, Citigroup (through subsidiaries such as Citibank, Salomon Smith Barney and Travelers) buys (and also helps underwrite or sell) World Bank bonds.[299]

International Development Association (IDA) was created in 1960 to provide long-term loans at zero interest to the poorest developing countries. The mission of IDA is "to support efficient and effective programs to reduce poverty and improve the quality of life in its poorest member countries." "IDA lends only to those countries that have a per capita income in 1999 of less than $885 and lack the financial ability to borrow from IBRD. At present, 78 countries are eligible to borrow from IDA. Together these countries are home to 2.3 billion people, comprising 53 percent of the total population of the developing countries." IDA funds projects that "protect the environment, improve conditions for private business, build needed infrastructure, and support reforms aimed at liberalizing countries' economies."[300]

Multilateral Guarantee Agency (MIGA) was created in 1988 "to encourage foreign direct investment into developing countries by providing political risk insurance against such risks as transfer restriction, expropriation, breach of contract, and war and civil disturbance, and by extending investment marketing services to host developing countries to assist them with more effective promotion of their own private investment opportunities." In other words, helping corporations penetrate foreign markets and insuring corporate profits from the political risks of those who live there.

Transfer restriction is defined as "an investor's inability to convert local currency (capital, interest, principal, profits, royalties and other remittances) into foreign exchange for transfer outside the host country." *Expropriation* is defined as "loss of the insured investment as a result of acts by the host government that may reduce or eliminate ownership of, control over, or rights to the insured investment. In addition to outright nationalization and confiscation, 'creeping' expropriation—a series of acts that, over time, have an expropriatory effect—is also covered."

MIGA insures corporate investments "against loss from damage to, or the destruction or disappearance of, tangible assets caused by politically-motivated acts of war or civil disturbance in the host country, including revolution, insurrection, coups d'état, sabotage, and terrorism."

Examples of MIGA insurance in 1999:

- MIGA insured the American-based corporation El Paso Energy's investment in the construction and operation of a 3,150 kilometer natural gas pipeline from Santa Cruz (Bolivia) to Porto Alegre (Brazil) against the risks of transfer restriction, expropriation, war and civil disturbance. The project has also received a $130 million World Bank loan and a $240 million loan from Inter-American Development Bank.
- MIGA has insured the International Paper Company's equity investment in a pulp and paper mill near St. Petersburg, Russia. The $30 million guarantee covers the investment against the risks of transfer restriction, expropriation, war and civil disturbance.
- MIGA has issued $40 million in guarantees to Citibank for a shareholder loan to its branch bank in Caracas, Venezuela. The guarantee covers the loan against the risks of transfer restriction and expropriation. "The loan will allow Citibank, N.A. (Venezuela) to expand its services to local and multinational

companies in the areas of oil and petrochemicals, metal and mining, and telecommunications. The branch provides trade financing, short and medium-term U.S. dollar financing, foreign exchange services transactions, and development of capital market products."

WORLD BUSINESS COUNCIL FOR SUSTAINABLE DEVELOPMENT

CHEMIN DE CONCHES
1231 CONCHES-GENEVA
SWITZERLAND
P 41 22 839 3100
WWW.WBCSD.ORG

World Business Council for Sustainable Development was created in 1995 from the merger of Business Council for Sustainable Development (BCSD) of Geneva and the World Industry Council for the Environment (WBCE) of Paris, which was an International Chamber of Commerce (ICC) initiative.

The BCSD was founded by Swiss billionaire Stephan Schmidheiny at the request of Maurice Strong, the secretary-general of the 1992 United Nations Conference on the Environment and Development (UNCED), also known as the Rio Earth Summit. BCSD was the corporate front group that distributed the greenwash classic *Changing Course: A Global Business Perspective on Development and the Environment* at Rio. Greenpeace attacked BCSD at Rio by countering with the *Greenpeace Book of Greenwash*, which explains how BCSD was formed in 1990 by 48 CEOs of chemical, forestry and pesticide corporations, and how it was interlocked with the International Chamber of Commerce *(see profile of ICC on page 87)*. BCSD hired the greenwash experts at the Burson-Marsteller public relations firm to help lead the fight to preempt binding international agreements for environmental protection at Rio.[301]

The merged organization, WBCSD, consists of 120 international corporations from thirty countries, spread across twenty industrial sectors. Its purpose is stated to be "closer co-operation between business, governments, NGOs and other organisations concerned with sustainable development," and to be "the leading business advocate on issues connected with the environment and sustainable development."[302]

In October 2000, the WBCSD website listed 156 corporate members, including ABB Asea Brown Boveri, Alcoa, Anglo American, Aracruz Celulose, Bayer, BP, Broken Hill Proprietary, Cargill, China Petro-

Chemical Corporation (SINOPEC), Conoco, Dow Chemical, DuPont, Fletcher Challenge, Ford Motor, General Motors, Imperial Chemical Industries, International Paper Company, Japan Atomic Power Company, Mitsubishi, Monsanto, Nestlé, Newmont Mining, Noranda, Norsk Hydro, Novartis, Phelps Dodge, Placer Dome, Rio Tinto, Shell International, Unocal and Weyerhaeuser.[303]

WBCSD has five sectoral projects on Forestry, Mining and Minerals, Cement, Mobility, and the Electrical Utility Industry.

The Sustainable Forest Industry Project is co-chaired by the CEOs of Westvaco and International Paper, with Aracruz Celulose and UPM-Kymmene (Finland) as vice chairs. Members include Companhia Vale do Rio Doce (Brazil), Mitsubishi (Japan), Shell International (UK), Stora Enso (Sweden), Procter & Gamble (USA), UBS (Switzerland), and Weyerhaeuser (USA). The "Forests Dialogue" consists of Nigel Sizer (World Resources Institute) and Scott Wallinger (WBCSD/Westvaco), Justin Stead (World Wildlife Fund), Steven Bass (IIED), Sergei Tsyplenkov (Greenpeace), Scott Rietbergen (IUCN), Jurgen Blaser (World Bank), Edward Markaroff (Russian Forest Industry), and Gary Dunning (Yale University Forest Forum).[304]

At EXPO 2000 in Hannover, the WBCSD Foundation co-sponsored a Virtual University mini-course on Sustainable Enterprise with CNN and ZERI Foundation.

With the World Bank, WBCSD co-sponsored a Leadership, Value and Competitiveness training for government and business leaders, academics and journalists in Sarajevo in June 2000. "The two organizations agreed . . . to a joint initiative to put business ethics at the heart of a new Internet-based educational project in the developing world."

In October 2000, WBCSD sponsored a Euro Environment 2000 forum in Aalborg, Denmark "for industry to interact with government and stakeholders in a constructive dialogue on environmental performance."

"The WBCSD is committed to Kofi Annan's Global Compact, proposing that business embrace a set of core, principles for human rights, workers' rights and environmental protection" *(see the profile of the United Nations for more on the Global Compact).*

WORLD ECONOMIC FORUM (DAVOS)

91-93 ROUTE DE LA CAPITE
CH-1223 COLOGNY
GENEVA, SWITZERLAND
P 41.22.869.1212
WWW.WEFORUM.ORG

Founded by business professor Klaus Schwab in 1970 as the European Management Forum, the World Economic Forum (WEF) is also known as "Davos," for the Swiss town in which annual meetings are held. WEF describes itself as "the foremost global partnership of business, political, intellectual and other leaders of society committed to improving the state of the world. Members, constituents and collaborators have a unique opportunity, through their association with the World Economic Forum, to engage in processes of developing and sharing ideas, opinions and knowledge on the key issues of the global agenda. The World Economic Forum is an independent, impartial, not-for-profit Foundation which acts in the spirit of entrepreneurship in the global public interest to further economic growth and social progress."[305] The theme of the 1996 meeting was "Sustaining Globalization."

WEF core membership consists of the 1,000 foremost global corporations; a second level of membership consists of smaller corporations. The WEF Council of forty prominent members meets twice a year.

The WEF annual meeting consists of workshops and informal

Davos, high up in the Swiss Alps, is not the center of a global capitalist conspiracy to divide up the world. Davos is where the global elite meets under the umbrella of the WEF to iron out a rough consensus on how to ideologically confront and defuse the challenges to the system. Meeting shortly after what many regarded as the cataclysm in Seattle, the Davos crew in late January composed the politically correct line. Repeated like a mantra by personalities like Bill Clinton, Tony Blair, Bill Gates, Nike CEO Phil Knight, and WEF guru Klaus Schwab, the chorus went this way: "Globalization is the wave of the future. But globalization is leaving the majority behind. Those voices spoke out in Seattle. It's time to bring the fruits of globalization and free trade to the many."

Walden Bello, at the demonstrations
against the World Economic Forum,
in Melbourne, Australia, September 2000

meetings to discuss global economic rules for finance, trade and development. In the 1970s WEF started Country Forums in which corporate executives were brought together with the government officials from various countries. WEF also sponsored ad hoc meetings such as an Arab-European Business Leaders Symposium and a Latin American-European Business Leaders Symposium. In the 1980s, WEF began to bring together the CEOs in ten different industry sectors (Automotive, Chemicals, Energy, Engineering and Construction, Entertainment, Finance, Food and Beverage, Information Technologies, Media, Communication and Entertainment, Retail and Consumer Goods, Transport Services, Travel and Tourism). In the 1990s, WEF worked on promoting the economic integration of Eastern and Central Europe and Latin America, and started a Global Leaders for Tomorrow forum and a World Art Forum.

In 1993 WEF began to limit its meetings to members and invited guests only. Media attendees are handpicked, and some have been refused accreditation after reporting critically about the WEF. A minimal number of NGOs are allowed to attend.

MEETINGS

A list of recent meetings organized by WEF throughout the world is given on its website.[307]

The power of capitalism to mediate the gap between rich and poor is pretty incredible. Indeed, I think, year by year, the gap gets less.

Microsoft chairman Bill Gates, at the 1997
World Economic Forum, Davos, Switzerland
(quoted in Seattle Weekly, *October 15, 1998)*

WORLD TRADE ORGANIZATION (WTO)

CENTRE WILLIAM RAPPARD
RUE DE LAUSANNE 154
CH-1211 GENEVA 21, SWITZERLAND
P 41.22.739.51.11
WWW.WTO.ORG

In 1995, fifty years after it was envisioned by corporate leaders and rejected by the world's nations, the World Trade Organization was established to provide a forum for future international trade negotiations and to implement and enforce global trade rules. The decision to create the WTO was made at the Uruguay Round of the General Agreement on Tariffs and Trade (GATT). GATT and twenty other international agreements have since been subsumed under the ambitious and authoritative WTO.

A group of corporations might gain political influence over a decision by lobbying national governments. A bank or group of banks might gain economic influence over an industry or a regional economy by extending or leveraging financial resources. The WTO is distinctly different from corporations and industry associations, because it has explicit authority under international law to decide which local and national laws are in violation of its trade rules.

In addition to negotiating binding agreements on trade in specific industries such as agriculture, textiles, and services, the WTO also "aims to provide a comprehensive legal framework for the international trading system." WTO member countries agree not to take unilateral action, but to submit disputes to the WTO, whose Director-General asks the General Council, convened as the Dispute Settlement Body (DSB), to establish an independent panel to examine each case.[308] WTO tribunal members in cases already heard have included Arthur Dunkel (Nestle, GATT, International Chamber of Commerce) and Warren Christopher (U.S. Department of State, Council on Foreign Relations, Lockheed Martin, First Interstate Bank, Carnegie).

The income share of the richest 20 per cent of the world's population rose from 69 to 83 per cent between 1965 and 1990.

UN Commission on Trade and Development (UNCTAD),
Inequality and Poverty Trends, January 2000

The WTO has ruled against every environmental law it has reviewed, and its decisions have resulted in weakening of the environmental and health and safety standards of several nations.[309]

- The WTO ruled that the U.S. Clean Air Act violates trade rules; in response, the U.S. EPA weakened its regulations limiting gasoline contaminants.
- The WTO ruled against the U.S. Endangered Species Act provisions requiring shrimp sold in the U.S. to be caught with devices that protect sea turtles.
- The WTO ruled against the European ban on selling beef with hormone residues, and imposed $116 million in sanctions when the EU refused to accept tainted meat.
- The WTO ruled against Australia's laws regarding the import of raw salmon.
- The WTO struck down a Massachusetts law rejecting purchases from corporations doing business with the military regime in Burma; WTO trade rules forbid the consideration of non-commercial factors such as human rights in government purchasing decisions. In some cases, even a threat to bring a case before the WTO results in the gutting of laws protecting human rights, health and safety.
- While the Massachusetts-Burma case was being heard, Maryland was considering a similar law regarding human rights in Nigeria, but federal lobbying and the threat of another WTO ruling contributed to the defeat of the proposed legislation in Maryland.
- The U.S. weakened its dolphin-safe tuna regulations when Mexico threatened to sue.
- The U.S. and EU have threatened to go to the WTO if new fuel efficiency standards are legislated.
- South Korea had a policy of allowing meat to sit on shelves for no more than 30 days, but extended it to 90 days to avoid a WTO challenge from the United States.

The WTO's 134 member nations are controlled by the most powerful economies. At GATT meetings in Uruguay and Singapore, the U.S., European Union, Canada and Japan invited a few selected countries

---

In 1965, personal income in the richest seven countries was twenty times higher than in the twenty poorest countries; in 1995, the income of the rich was 39 times greater than that of the poor.

UN Commission on Trade and Development (UNCTAD),
Trade and Development Report, 1997

into "green rooms" to negotiate trade deals, leaving the majority of the members out of the decision making. The dominant nations promised to conduct the WTO ministerial in Seattle in November 1999 in a more open and democratic fashion, but once again, numerous countries protested the use of green rooms to control the WTO. In a letter to the WTO chairman, the protesting nations declared that "[e]fficiency may suffer. Arbitrary exclusion is not an option."[310]

DIRECTORS-GENERAL OF GATT / WTO

- Sir Eric Wyndham White (GATT, 1948–68). British Treasury, UNRRA, Emergency Economic Committee for Europe, Preparatory Committee for the International Trade Organization, Havana Conference.
- Olivier Long (GATT, 1968–80). Swiss Federal Political Department and Division of Commerce, Swiss Legation in Washington, European Free Trade Association, Swiss Ambassador to UK.
- Arthur Dunkel (GATT, 1980–93). Nestle, International Chamber of Commerce, WTO dispute panelist.
- Peter Sutherland (GATT/WTO, 1993–95). Attorney General of Ireland, Member of the Council of State, European Commissioner, chairman or director of Allied Irish Banks, BP Amoco, and Goldman Sachs.
- Renato Ruggiero (WTO, 1995–99). Italian diplomat, Italian Director-General of Economic Affairs, Secretary-General of the Ministry of Foreign Affairs, Minister for Foreign Trade, director of FIAT, Kissinger Associates, Booz Allen, and other Italian and European corporations.
- Michael Moore (WTO, 1999-present). Former New Zealand Minister of Overseas Trade and Marketing, Minister of Tourism, Sport and Recreation (1984-1987), Minister of Foreign Affairs (1990), Deputy Minister of Finance (1988-1990), and Prime Minister.

Forthcoming meetings are posted at the WTO's website.

The WTO's . . . authority stems from its ability to strike down the domestic laws, programs, and policies of its member nations and to compel them to establish new laws that conform to WTO rules. This authority extends beyond the national government level, all the way to provinces, states, counties, and cities.

Debi Barker and Jerry Mandar, Invisible Government, *International Forum on Globalization, 1999*

CORPORATE LOBBYING
RANKED BY EXPENDITURES[311]

	1999 Lobbying Expenditures	1998 Lobbying Expenditures	1998 Lobbying Expenditures
Chamber of Commerce of the US	$ 18,760,000	$ 17,000,000	$ 14,240,000
American Medical Assn	18,180,000	16,820,000	17,280,000
Philip Morris	14,820,000	23,148,000	16,248,000
American Hospital Assn	12,480,000	10,520,000	7,880,000
Exxon Mobil Corp	11,695,800	11,960,000	10,454,660
Edison Electric Institute	11,580,000	11,020,000	10,020,000
Blue Cross/Blue Shield	11,162,354	9,171,572	8,761,936
SBC Communications	9,500,000	5,280,000	6,220,000
Schering-Plough Corp	9,231,000	4,268,000	2,682,508
AT&T	8,560,000	7,950,000	8,110,000
Ford Motor Co	8,360,000	13,807,000	7,343,000
General Electric	8,318,024	7,630,000	7,440,000
Business Roundtable	8,300,000	11,640,000	9,480,000
Boeing Co	8,200,000	8,440,000	10,020,000
Sprint Corp	7,951,711	7,398,665	6,740,000
United Services Auto Assn Group	7,470,000	3,520,000	3,560,000
Natl Cmte to Preserve Social Security	7,220,000	6,780,000	7,660,000
General Motors	7,017,874	8,414,900	10,600,000
Abbott Laboratories	6,789,000	1,877,147	893,300
National Assn of Realtors	6,760,000	6,040,000	6,320,000
American Council of Life Insurance	6,600,000	7,050,000	4,935,000
GTE Corp	6,490,000	4,200,000	3,880,000
IBM Corp	6,360,000	5,552,000	5,240,000
Securities Industry Assn	6,059,277	4,660,000	5,000,000
Fannie Mae	6,000,000	5,550,000	4,960,000

TOP LOBBYISTS AND THEIR CLIENTS

The top industries in order are pharmaceuticals-health products, insurance, electric utilities, oil and gas, telephone utilities, computers, health professionals, business associations, and air transport.

In 1998, 128 lobbying firms reported at least $1 million in income. This table lists the top fifteen.[313]

Lobbying Firm	1999 Receipts	Top Clients
Cassidy & Associates	$ 20,840,000	Boston University United Space Alliance Rush-Presbyterian- St Lukes Medical Ctr Montefiore Medical Center Ocean Spray Cranberries General Dynamics
Patton Boggs	17,790,000	Pacific Lumber & Shipping Assn of Trial Lawyers of America Mars Inc Dole Food Co Soros Private Equity Partners
Verner, Liipfert	15,950,000	Puerto Rico Industrial Development Evans International Ltd Lockheed Martin Visa USA SBC Communications
Akin, Gump	13,280,000	AT&T Pohang Iron & Steel Gila River Indian Community PG&E Corp Volkswagen AG
Preston, Gates	11,620,000	Mississippi Band of Choctaw Indians Western Pacific Economic Council Channel One Network Pitney Bowes Inc US Maritime Coalition

Lobbying Firm	1999 Receipts
PricewaterhouseCoopers	$ 10,130,000
Williams & Jensen	8,820,000
Washington Counsel	8,470,000
Hogan & Hartson	8,353,056
Van Scoyoc Associates	8,090,000
Barbour, Griffith & Rogers	7,460,000
Podesta.com	6,700,000
Dutko Group	6,502,450
Arnold & Porter	6,265,000
Hooper, Owen	6,091,000

"These guys are not ordinary lobbyists; they constitute the elite of the influence salesmen who stick around the nation's capital year after year, Congress after Congress, administration after administration—a group of people so self-confident and secure in their access to political power that, unlike many other Washington players, they actually strive to keep their names out of the paper. In their rarified stratum, satisfaction comes from getting the job done quietly and effectively. The client is supposed to get the credit; the lobbyists gets the money—usually a great deal of money."

John R. MacArthur, The Selling of Free Trade

TOP POLITICAL DONORS TO U.S.
POLITICAL CAMPAIGNS, 1989-2002[314]

American Federation of State, County & Municipal Employees	$ 33,374,308
National Education Assn	22,343,233
National Assn of Realtors	21,995,021
Assn of Trial Lawyers of America	21,370,267
American Medical Assn	19,565,459
Philip Morris	19,432,838
Carpenters & Joiners Union	19,401,587
Teamsters Union	19,333,583
Intl Brotherhood of Electrical Workers	19,304,159
Communications Workers of America	18,905,478
United Auto Workers	18,468,671
AT&T	18,055,862
Laborers Union	17,814,959
American Federation of Teachers	17,799,549
United Food & Commercial Workers Union	17,345,335
Machinists & Aerospace Workers Union	16,772,053
Service Employees International Union	16,766,994
Citigroup Inc	15,258,119
United Parcel Service	15,089,009
National Auto Dealers Assn	15,028,585
Goldman Sachs	14,539,491
National Assn of Letter Carriers	13,709,792
National Rifle Assn	13,689,994
AFL-CIO	13,421,310
National Assn of Home Builders	13,112,272
American Bankers Assn	12,319,589
AOL Time Warner	12,180,620
FedEx Corp	11,995,086
BellSouth Corp	11,340,319
SBC Communications	11,102,440

\ **TOP GLOBAL CORPORATIONS BY INDUSTRY**

These are the 500 largest corporations in the world, listed by industry and then ranked by size of 2001 revenues. Each corporation's sales, profits, and other data are available online from *Fortune (www.fortune.com)*. Other rankings of U.S. and global corporations are available online from *Forbes (www.forbes.com)* and from *Business Week (www.businessweek.com)*.

Aerospace and Defense
Boeing
United Technologies
EADS
Lockheed Martin
Honeywell Intl.
Raytheon
Bombardier
Northrop Grumman
BAE Systems
Textron
General Dynamics

Airlines
AMR
United Airlines
Lufthansa Group
Delta Air Lines
Japan Airlines
British Airways
Air France Group

Banks: Commercial and Savings
Deutsche Bank
Credit Suisse
BNP Paribas
Bank of America Corp.
J.P. Morgan Chase
UBS
HSBC Holding PLC
Mizuho Holdings
Fortis
ABN AMRO Holding
HypoVereinsbank
Crédit Agricole
Royal Bank of Scotland
Santander Central
  Hispano Group

Sumitomo Mitsui Banking
HBOS
Barclays
Wells Fargo
Mitsubishi Tokyo
  Financial Group
DZ Bank
UFJ Holdings
Bank One Corp.
Société Générale
Banco Bilbao Vizcaya
  Argentaria
Commerzbank
Westdeutsche
  Landesbank
Lloyds TSB Group
Wachovia Corp.
Rabobank
IntesaBci
Industrial & Commercial
  Bank of China
FleetBoston
Dexia Group
Crédit Lyonnais
Almanij
Bank Of China
Abbey National
Washington Mutual
Landesbank
  Baden-Wurttemberg
Groupe Caisse d'Épargne
Royal Bank of Canada
National Australia Bank
U.S. Bancorp
Bayerische Landesbank
UniCredito Italiano
Banco Bradesco
Canadian Imperial
  Bank of Commerce
Bank of Nova Scotia

Toronto-Dominion Bank
China Construction Bank
Norinchukin Bank
Nordea
Banco Do Brasil
Bank of Montreal
Danske Bank Group
Daiwa Bank Holdings
Agricultural Bank of China
Bankgesellschaft Berlin
Norddeutsche Landesb.
Kreditanstalt für
  Wiederaufbau
Itaæsa-Investimentos Itaæ
MBNA

Beverages
PepsiCo
Coca-Cola
Diageo
Coca-Cola
Anheuser-Busch
Suntory

Building Materials, Glass
Saint-Gobain
Lafarge
Asahi Glass

Chemicals
BASF
Dow Chemical
Bayer
DuPont de Nemours (E.I.)
Mitsubishi Chemical
Akzo Nobel

**Computer and
Data Services**
Electronic Data Systems
Computer Sciences

Computer Software
Microsoft
Oracle

**Computers,
Office Equipment**
Intl. Business Machines
Hewlett-Packard
Fujitsu
Compaq Computer
Dell Computer
Canon
Sun Microsystems
Xerox
Ricoh

Diversified Financials
General Electric
Citigroup
Fannie Mae
Freddie Mac
American Express
Household International

**Diversified
Outsourcing Services**
Adecco
Accenture
Manpower

**Electronics,
Electrical Equipment**
Siemens
Hitachi
Sony
Matsushita
  Electric Industrial
Toshiba
NEC
Tyco International
Samsung Electronics
Mitsubishi Electric
Royal Philips Electronics
ABB
LG Electronics
Sanyo Electric
Emerson Electric
Sharp
Electrolux

Sumitomo
  Electric Industries
Whirlpool

Energy
Enron
American Electric Power
Duke Energy
El Paso
Rwe
Reliant Energy
Dynegy
China National Petroleum
Aquila
Suez
Mirant
Gazprom
CMS Energy
Cinergy
TransCanada Pipelines
Williams
Allegheny Energy

**Engineering,
Construction**
Bouygues
Kajima
Vinci
Skanska
Taisei
Shimizu
Obayashi
Sekisui House
Takenaka

Entertainment
Vivendi Universal
AOL Time Warner
Walt Disney
Viacom
News Corp.

Food and Drug Stores
Carrefour
Royal Ahold
Kroger
Metro
Albertson's
Safeway
Tesco
Ito-Yokado
Walgreen
J. Sainsbury
AEON

Groupe Auchan
CVS
Delhaize 'Le Lion'
George Weston
Publix Super Markets
Rite Aid
Winn-Dixie Stores
Coles Myer
Safeway
Migros
Woolworths
Great Atl. & Pacific Tea

**Food Consumer
Products**
Nestlé
Unilever
ConAgra
Sara Lee
Groupe Danone

Food Production
Archer Daniels Midland
Edison
Farmland Industries
Tyson Foods

Food Services
McDonald's
Compass Group
Sodexho Alliance

**Forest and
Paper Products**
International Paper
Georgia-Pacific
Weyerhaeuser
Stora Enso

General Merchandisers
Wal-Mart Stores
Sears Roebuck
Target
Kmart
J.C. Penney
Groupe Pinault-Printemps
Foncière Euris
Daiei
Federated Dept. Stores
KarstadtQuelle
May Dept. Stores
Marks & Spencer

Health Care

Aetna
UnitedHealth Group
Cigna
HCA
AdvancePCS
WellPoint Health Netwks.
Tenet Healthcare
PacifiCare Health
Anthem
Humana

Household and Personal Products

Procter & Gamble
Kimberly-Clark
L'Oréal
Henkel

Industrial and Farm Equipment

Thyssen Krupp
Mitsubishi
  Heavy Industries
Alstom
Caterpillar
Deere

Insurance: Life, Health (mutual)

Nippon Life Insurance
Dai-ichi Mutual
  Life Insurance
Asahi Mutual
  Life Insurance
Sumitomo Life Insurance
New York Life Insurance
Meiji Life Insurance
TIAA-CREF
Mitsui Mutual
  Life Insurance
Mass. Mutual Life Ins.
Standard Life Assurance
Yasuda Mutual
  Life Insurance
Northwestern Mutual
Taiyo Mutual
  Life Insurance
Daido Life Insurance

Insurance: Life, Health (stock)

ING Group
AXA
Aviva
Assicurazioni Generali
Prudential
MetLife
Aegon
Prudential Financial
CNP Assurances
Samsung Life Insurance
Legal & General
Swiss Life Ins. & Pension
Power Corp. of Canada
Cathay Life
Old Mutual
Sun Life
  Financial Services
Manulife Financial

Insurance: P and C (mutual)

State Farm Insurance
Liberty Mutual Group
Groupama

Insurance: P and C (stock)

Allianz
American Intl. Group
Munich Re Group
Zurich Financial Services
Berkshire Hathaway
Allstate
Royal & Sun Alliance
Swiss Reinsurance
Loews
Tokio Marine &
  Fire Insurance
Mitsui Sumitomo
  Insurance
Hartford Fin.
  Services Nationwide
Yasuda Fire &
  Marine Insurance

Mail, Package, Freight Delivery

U.S. Postal Service
Deutsche Post
United Parcel Service
Japan Postal Service
FedEx

La Poste
Nippon Express
Consignia

Metals

Alcoa
Nippon Steel
Norsk Hydro
NKK
Arcelor
Alcan
Arbed
Corus Group
Sumitomo
  Metal Industries
POSCO

Mining, Crude-Oil Production

Pemex
BHP Billiton
Anglo American
Occidental Petroleum
RAG
Lukoil

Miscellaneous

Dior (Christian)
Dentsu
Marriott International
3M
TUI
Waste Management
Wolseley

Motor Vehicles and Parts

General Motors
Ford Motor
DaimlerChrysler
Toyota Motor
Volkswagen
Honda Motor
Fiat
Nissan Motor
Peugeot
BMW
Renault
Hyundai Motor
Robert Bosch
Delphi
Mitsubishi Motors
Denso
Johnson Controls

Volvo
Visteon
Bridgestone
Mazda Motor
TRW
Michelin
Man Group
Goodyear Tire & Rubber
Lear
Suzuki Motor
Isuzu Motors
Magna International
Fuji Heavy Industries
Dana

Network and Other Communications Equipment
Motorola
Nokia
Lucent Technologies
L.M. Ericsson
Cisco Systems
Nortel Networks

Oil and Gas Equipment, Services
Schlumberger
Halliburton

Petroleum Refining
Exxon Mobil
British Petroleum
Royal Dutch/Shell
ChevronTexaco
Total Fina Elf
PDVSA
ENI
Sinopec
Repsol YPF
Marathon Oil
SK
Conoco
Statoil
Petrobrás
Phillips Petroleum
Nippon Mitsubishi Oil
Indian Oil
Petronas
Idemitsu Kosan
Valero Energy
Amerada Hess
Japan Energy
Sunoco

Chinese Petroleum
Cosmo Oil
Showa Shell Sekiyu

Pharmaceuticals
Merck
Johnson & Johnson
Pfizer
GlaxoSmithKline
Bristol-Myers Squibb
Aventis
Pharmacia
Novartis
Roche Group
AstraZeneca
Abbott Laboratories
Wyeth
Eli Lilly

Publishing, Printing
Bertelsmann
Lagardère Groupe
Dai Nippon Printing
Toppan Printing

Railroads
East Japan Railway
SNCF
Deutsche Bahn
Union Pacific
Central Japan Railway

Scientific, Photo, Control Equipment
Fuji Photo Film
Eastman Kodak

Securities
Morgan Stanley
Merrill Lynch
Goldman Sachs Group
Lehman Brothers Hldgs.

Semiconductors and Other Electronic Components
Intel
Solectron
Onex
Flextronics International

Specialty Retailers
Home Depot
Costco

Lowe's
AutoNation
Best Buy
Kingfisher
Gap
Otto Versand
Circuit City
Office Depot
Toys 'R' Us
LVMH
Staples
TJX

Telecommunications
Nippon Telegraph
  & Telephone
Verizon Communications
AT&T
SBC Communications
Deutsche Telekom
France Télécom
WorldCom
Vodafone
BT
Olivetti
Telefónica
Sprint
BellSouth
Alcatel
KDDI
China Telecommunications
Qwest Communications
China Mobile
  Communications
BCE
Japan Telecom
Telstra
KT
Carso Global Telecom
Royal KPN

Tobacco
Philip Morris
British American Tobacco
Japan Tobacco

Trading
Mitsubishi
Mitsui
Itochu
Sumitomo
Marubeni
E. ON
Nissho Iwai

Samsung
Hyundai
LG International
Tomen
Toyota Tsusho
SK Global
Nichimen
Sinochem
COFCO

Utilities:
Gas and Electric
State Power
Tokyo Electric Power
Électricité De France
TXU
Enel
PG&E Corp.
Kansai Electric Power
Centrica
Chubu Electric Power
Korea Electric Power
Exelon
Xcel Energy
Endesa
Tohoku Electric Power
Gaz de France
Edison International
Kyushu Electric Power
Dominion Resources
Southern

Wholesalers:
Electronics and
Office Equipment
Ingram Micro
Tech Data
Avnet
Arrow Electronics

Wholesalers:
Food and Grocery
Sysco
Supervalu
Fleming

Wholesalers:
Health Care
McKesson
Cardinal Health
Franz Haniel
AmerisourceBergen
Alliance Unichem

RECENT STUDIES OF CORPORATE SUBSIDIES

Source	Year	Title of Report	Summary/Conclusions
Friends of the Earth et al.	Annual	Green Scissors	Case studies of pork barrel subsidies to polluting industries.
Wilderness Society and Environmental Defense Fund	1993	The Living Landscape: Volume 3: Taxpayers' Double Burden	Recovery of wildlife species endangered due to unsustainable natural resource extraction on federal lands would cost between $72 million and $136 million per year.
Essential Information	1994	Aid for Dependent Corporations: Federal Estimates of Corporate Welfare for 1994	In 1994, taxpayers spent $51 billion in direct subsidies and $53 billion in tax breaks.
Federation for Industrial Retention & Renewal and Grassroots Policy Project	1989, 1994	No More Candy Store: States and Cities Making Job Subsidies Accountable	Describes billions of dollars worth of corporate subsidies from local, state, and federal governments.
Progressive Policy Institute of the Democratic Party	1994	Cut-and-Invest to Compete and Win: A Budget Strategy for American Growth	$114 billion in expenditures and $111 billion in tax breaks could be replaced with $100 billion in more productive public investment.
U.S. House Committee on Natural Resources, Subcommittee on Oversight and Investigations	1994	Taking from the Taxpayer: Public Subsidies for Natural Resource Development	Examines subsidies to mining, timber, irrigation, hydropower, grazing, and recreation. Concludes that federal programs are inconsistent, are not based on need, and do not consider the effects on the economy or environment.
Cato Institute	1995	Ending Corporate Welfare As We Know It	In 1995, more than $85 billion was spent to subsidize private businesses.
U.S. Public Interest Research Group	1996	Feeding at the Trough: Campaign Contributions and Taxpayer Handouts for Polluters	From 1989 to mid-1995, PACs representing industries that pollute contributed $47 million to candidates who provided $23 billion in subsidies.

U.S. House Budget Committee hearing	March 7, 1996	*Corporate Welfare*	Gathers a few statistics and lots of rhetoric on the various subsidies to business.
Public Information Network	1997	*Matrix of Energy & Transportation Studies*	Summarizes subsidies to the auto, coal, nuclear, oil, and other industries.
Time Magazine series by Donald Barlett and James Steele	November 1998	*Special Report on Corporate Welfare*	Anecdotal accounts of federal, state, and local government handouts to corporations.

The following table lists selected committee, advisory group and other leaders of the Bilderberg group from 1982 to the present. Roles listed as beginning in 1982 may actually have begun earlier.[315]

Name	Interlocks with Government and Corporations	Role in Bilderberg	Years
Umberto Agnelli	Fiat, Allianz, Istituto Finanziario Industrial, Salomon Smith Barney, Italy–Japan Business Group, Trilateral Commission	Steering Committee	1994-98
Paul A. Allaire	Chairman of Xerox, Director of Sara Lee, NY Stock Exchange, SmithKline Beecham, member of Business Council and Business Roundtable	Steering Committee	1994-98
George W. Ball	Banker, lawyer, diplomat, U.S. Under-Secretary of State (died 1994)	Advisory Group	1982-93
Francisco Pinto Balsemao	New University of Lisbon, Chairman of Impressa, Prime Minister of Portugal	Steering Committee	1989-98
Christoph Bertram	Director of Foundation on Science & Policy, correspondent for Die Zeit	Steering Committee	1989-98
Selahattin Beyazit	Turkish businessman, Galatasaray Club	Steering Committee	1982-98
Conrad M. Black	Major media owner, Hollinger, Argus, Ravelston, EdperBrascan, Jerusalem Post, Sterling Newspapers, Sotheby's, UniMédia, The Telegraph	Steering Committee	1990-98
William P. Bundy	Former editor of Foreign Affairs, the journal of Council on Foreign Affairs	Advisory Group	1982-98
Costa Carras	Europa Nostra, Union of Greek Shipowners, Association for Democracy in the Balkans, Business Advisory Council to Southeastern Europe Cooperative Initiative	Steering Committee	1982-94
Peter Carrington	Former British Foreign Secretary, Secretary General of NATO, Chairman of Christies	Chairman	1989-98

Name	Description	Role	Years
Jaime Carvajal Urquijo	Banco Urquijo, Banco Hispano, SGS Spain, Iberfomento, Ford España, Ericsson S.A, Kleinwort Benson Group, Asland, Plus Ultra, Agroman, Abengoa Spain-US Council, Prado Museum, Trilateral Commission	Steering Committee	1989–98
Etienne Davignon	Chairman of Societe Generale de Belgique, former Vice Chair of European Commission	Steering Committee Chairman	1989–98 1999–
Theodore L. Eliot, Jr.	Dean Emeritus of Fletcher School of Law, former U.S. Ambassador	Secretary General	1982–93
Anthony Griffin	Director of Guardian Group	Advisory Group	1982–98
Victor Halberstadt	Professor of public economics at Leiden University	Secretary General	1982–99
Westye Halberstadt	Chairman of Leif Hoegh, former president of the Norwegian Shipowners Association	Steering Committee	1993–98
Vernon E. Jordan, Jr.	NAACP, National Urban League, Akin Gump, Lazard Frères, Xerox, Dow Jones, Union Carbide, CFR, Trialteral Commission	Steering Committee	1982–98
Henry A. Kissinger	Former U.S. Secretary of State, Director of Freeport McMoran and other corporations	Steering Committee	1982–98
Max Kohnstamm	European Policy Center, former Secretary-General of Action Committee for Europe	Advisory Group	1982–98
Pieter Korteweg	CEO of Robeco Group	Treasurer	1992–98
Marie-Josée Kravis (nee Drouin)	Senior fellow at Hudson Institute	Steering Committee	1989–98
André Levy-Lang	Former Chairman of Banque Paribas	Steering Committee	1994–98

Name	Interlocks with Government and Corporations	Role in Bilderberg	Years
David de Pury	Chairman of de Pury Pictet Turrettini & Company, former Co-Chairman of ABB	Steering Committee	1993–98
David Rockefeller	Chase Manhattan Bank, Trilateral Commission	Advisory Group	1982–98
Eric Roll (Lord Roll of Ipsden)	Warburg bank (now part of UBS)	Advisory Group	1982–98
Renato Ruggiero	Vice Chair of Schroder Salomon Smith Barney, former Director-General of WTO	Steering Committee	1993–98
Toger Seidenfaden	Editor of Politiken A/S, DanishTV2	Steering Committee	1994–98
Jack Sheinkman	Former President of the Amalgamated Textile Workers Union (AFL–CIO)	Steering Committee	1994–98
Peter D. Sutherland	Former Director-General of GATT, former European Commissioner, Chairman or Director of Goldman Sachs, BP Amoco, Allied Irish Banks, and Goldman Sachs	Steering Committee	1993–98
J. Martin Taylor	WH Smith Group, Goldman Sachs	Steering Committee	1994–98
James D. Wolfensohn	President of World Bank	Steering Committee	1993–98
Otto Wolff von Amerongen	CEO of Otto Wolff GmbH	Advisory Group	1982–98
Casimir A. Yost	Director of Georgetown University Institute for the Study of Diplomacy	Secretary General	1994–96

OFFICERS & DIRECTORS OF THE COUNCIL ON FOREIGN RELATIONS

LESLIE H. GELB, director of policy planning and arms control for international security affairs at the U.S. Department of Defense, and director of the Pentagon Papers Project, 1967-69, Brookings Institution fellow 1969 to 1973, journalist and columnist for 20 years at the *New York Times*, now trustee for the Carnegie Endowment for International Peace and Tufts University, director of Columbia University School of International and Public Affairs, advisory board member for the Center on Press, Politics and Public Policy at Harvard University's John F. Kennedy School of Government.

JESSICA P. EINHORN, visiting fellow at the International Monetary Fund, former managing director, vice president and treasurer of the World Bank from 1996-98, served in the U.S. Treasury, the U.S. State Department, and the U.S. International Development Cooperation Agency, director of Pitney Bowes.

LOUIS V. GERSTNER JR., CEO of IBM and RJR Nabisco, director of American Express, McKinsey & Co., Bristol-Myers Squibb, Memorial Sloan-Kettering Cancer Center, American Express, AT&T, Caterpillar, New York Times, Lincoln Center for the Performing Arts, the America China Society, U.S. President's National Security Telecommunications Advisory Committee, and Smithsonian Institution.

MAURICE R. GREENBERG, CEO of American International Group, Inc. (AIG), member of The Business Roundtable, member of the U.S. President's Advisory Committee for Trade Policy and Negotiations, chairman of the Center for Strategic and International Studies, chairman of U.S.-China Business Council, trustee of The Asia Society, founding chairman of the U.S.-Philippine Business Committee, chairman of Starr Foundation.

GEORGE J. MITCHELL, former U.S. Senator, now with law firm of Verner, Liipfert, Bernhard, McPherson and Hand, director of Walt Disney Company, Federal Express, Xerox, UNUM Insurance, KTI Inc., Staples, and Starwood Hotels and Resorts; and chairman of the International Crisis Group, the International Commission on Disarmament in Northern Ireland, the Peace Talks in Northern Ireland, the Ethics Committee of the U.S. Olympic Committee, and the Pew Charitable Foundation's National Health Care Commission.

WARREN B. RUDMAN, former U.S. Senator, founding co-chairman of the Concord Coalition, partner in the law firm Paul, Weiss, Rifkind, Wharton, and Garrison, U.S. President's Foreign Intelligence Advisory Board, trustee of Boston College, Valley Forge Military Academy, the Brookings Institution, and the Aspen Institute.

LEE CULLUM, syndicated columnist and television commentator, director of the Pacific Council on International Policy, the American Council on Germany, and the Inter-American Dialogue.

MARIO L. BAEZA, CEO of TCW/Latin America Partners, managing director of the Trust Company of the West, director of NAACP Legal Defense and Educational Fund, New York Philharmonic-Symphony Society, Jazz at Lincoln Center, and U.S. Cuba Trade and Economic Council.

THOMAS R. DONAHUE, Secretary-Treasurer of the AFL-CIO from 1979 to 1995, U.S. Assistant Secretary of Labor for Labor-Management Relations under Johnson, chairman of the U.S. Special Trade Representative's Labor Advisory Committee from 1989 to 1995, member of the President's Council on Sustainable Development, director of the National Endowment for Democracy, the American Arbitration Association, the Work in America Institute, and the National Planning Association.

PETER G. PETERSON, chairman of the private investment banking firm Blackstone Group, former chairman of Lehman Brothers Kuhn Loeb, chairman of the Federal Reserve Bank of New York, U.S. Secretary of Commerce 1972-73, director or former director of Transtar and Sony, 3M, Federated Department Stores, Black & Decker, General Foods, RCA, Continental Group, Cities Service, and UCAR International, founding chairman of the Institute for International Economics, trustee of Committee for Economic Development, the Japan Society, the Museum of Modern Art, director of the National Bureau of Economic Research, the Public Agenda Foundation, and the Nixon Center, and founding President of the Concord Coalition.

ROBERT B. ZOELLICK, U.S. Trade Representative, former CEO of the Center for Strategic and International Studies, John M. Olin Professor of National Security Affairs at the U.S. Naval Academy, executive vice president at Fannie Mae, Counselor of the U.S. Department of State, Deputy Chief of Staff at the White House, U.S. Department of the Treasury in various positions, director of Alliance Capital, Jones Intercable, and Said Holdings, member of Enron Corporation's Advisory Council, director of the Aspen Institute's Strategy Group on Foreign Policy, the German Marshall Fund of the U.S., the Overseas

BETTE BAO LORD, novelist, director of Radio Free Asia, trustee of Freedom House, and wife of former U.S. ambassador to China and U.S. State Department official Winston Lord.

VINCENT A. MAI, chairman of AEA Investors (founded in 1969 by the Rockefeller, Harriman, and Mellon industrial families; other members have included the CEOs of major corporations such as AT&T, GE, GM, IBM), director of Fannie Mae.

MICHAEL H. MOSKOW, president of the Federal Reserve Bank of Chicago, former official with the U.S. Council of Economic Advisors, U.S. Department of Housing and Urban Development, U.S. Department of Labor, CEO of Velsicol Chemical, U.S. Deputy United States Trade Representative under Bush, and director of the National Bureau of Economic Research.

GARRICK UTLEY, reporter for NBC, ABC, and CNN.

JOHN DEUTCH, revolving door between Massachusetts Institute of Technology and U.S. Department of Defense since the 1960s, Deputy Secretary 1994-95, director of U.S. Central Intelligence Agency 1995-96, director of Perkin-Elmer, Schlumberger, Citicorp, and Science Applications and Instruments Corporation (SAIC).

CARLA A. HILLS, Hills & Company International Consultants, director of IBM, Standard Oil, American Airlines, American International Group, Chevron, Lucent Technologies, Time Warner, advisor to Center for Strategic and International Studies, vice chair of National Committee on U.S.-China Relations and U.S. China Business Council, member of the Trilateral Commission, U.S. Trade Representative 1989-93, chairman of Urban Institute 1983-88, member of the Reagan's Commission on Defense Management, chairman of American Bar Association Antitrust Section, Secretary of U.S. Department of Housing and Urban Development under Ford.

ROBERT D. HORMATS, vice chairman Goldman Sachs, National Security Council advisor to Henry Kissinger, Brent Scowcroft and Zbigniew Brzezinski, official with the U.S. Department of State and the office of U.S. Trade Representative, member of the Trilateral Commission, director of the Russian-American Enterprise Fund (now the U.S. Russia Investment Fund).

WILLIAM J. MCDONOUGH, president of the Federal Reserve Bank of New York, executive with First National Bank of Chicago, adviser to the World Bank and International Finance Corporation, and Inter-American Development Bank, was with U.S. State Department in 1960s, director of the Bank for International Settlements, chairman of the Basle Committee on Banking Supervision, director of the New York Philharmonic Orchestra, member of the Trilateral Commission, trustee of The Economic Club of New York.

THEODORE C. SORENSEN, partner at Paul, Weiss, Rifkind, Wharton & Garrison, specializing in international business and government transactions, director of the Twentieth Century Fund, policy adviser and legal counsel to Senator and President John F. Kennedy.

GEORGE SOROS, billionaire investor and head of foundations with 50 offices worldwide, employing 1,000 staff, and spending more than $300 million a year for the "development of open societies."

HONORARY OFFICERS AND DIRECTORS EMERITI

DOUGLAS DILLON, investment banker, member of the New York Stock Exchange 1931-36, director of the United States and Foreign Securities Corporation, director and chairman of Dillon, Read, appointed U.S. Secretary of the Treasury under Kennedy, Under Secretary of State under Eisenhower, instrumental in creation of Organization of American States, Organization for Economic Cooperation and Development, and Inter-American Development Bank, Alliance for Progress Program.

CARYL P. HASKINS, General Electric and MIT in the 1930-40s, Haskins Labs, director of DuPont, president of Carnegie Institution.

CHARLES McC. MATHIAS JR., U.S. House and Senate 1961-85, chairman of First American Bankshares, partner in the international law firm of Jones, Day, Reavis and Pogue, president of the North Atlantic Assembly (NATO parliamentarians).

DAVID ROCKEFELLER, chairman of Chase Manhattan Bank, founder of Trilateral Commission, chairman of Rockefeller Brothers Fund, member of Bilderberg, Business Council, Business Roundtable, etc.

ROBERT A. SCALAPINO, political science professor at the University of California Berkeley 1962-90, Institute of East Asian Studies, Social Science Research Council, National Endowment for the Humanities, the Henry Luce Foundation, Earhart Foundation, director of Pacific Forum-CSIS, founder and chairman of National Committee on U.S.-China Relations, trustee of The Asia Foundation and the Atlantic Council.

CYRUS R. VANCE, Secretary of the U.S. Army and Deputy Defense Secretary under Kennedy and Johnson, peace negotiator with North Vietnam, U.S. Secretary of State under Carter, envoy for United Nations

Secretaries General, director of New York Times, IBM, General Dynamics, Manufacturers Trust, Pan American Airways, Aetna, trustee of Mayo Foundation, Japan Society, chairman of American Ditchley Foundation, Public Agenda Foundation, the Federal Reserve Bank of New York, and the Rockefeller Foundation.

GLENN E. WATTS, former president of the Communications Workers of America, executive council of AFL-CIO, secretary of United Way, director of Common Cause, trustee of Ford Fund and Aspen Institute.

Bank Information Center
733 15th Street NW, Suite 1126
Washington, DC 20005
P   202.737.7752
F   202.737.1155
E-MAIL info@bicusa.org
www.bicusa.org

Provides information and strategic support to NGOs throughout the world on the projects, policies and practices of the World Bank and other multilateral development banks. BIC advocates for greater transparency, accountability and citizen participation.

International Centre for Trade and Sustainable Development
Chemin des Anémones 13
1219 Chatelaine
Geneva, Switzerland
P   41.22.917.8492
F   41.22.917.8093
ww.ictsd.org

Publishes *BRIDGES Weekly Trade News Digest*, which tracks governmental, industry, and NGO meetings and conferences on trade and development.

Center for Public Integrity
910 17th Street NW, 7th floor
Washington, DC 20006
P   202.466.1300
F   202.466.1101
www.publicintegrity.org

Exposes conflicts of interest and money in politics through its book *The Buying of the President* (1996 and 2000 editions).

Center for Responsive Politics
1101 14th Street NW, Suite 1030
Washington, DC 20005
P   202.857.0044
F   202.857.7809
E-MAIL info@crp.org
www.crp.org *or*
www.opensecrets.org

Tracks money in politics and its effect on elections and public policy. Conducts computer-based research on campaign finance issues for the news media, academics, activists, and the public at large. The Center's work is aimed at creating a more educated voter, an involved citizenry and a more responsive government.

Common Cause
1250 Connecticut Avenue NW
Washington, DC 20036
P 202.833.1200
www.commoncause.org

Promotes honesty and integrity in government, and focuses on campaign finance and ethics reform. Maintains a website that tracks money in politics.

Corporate Europe Observatory
Paulus Potterstraat 20
1071 DA Amsterdam
Netherlands
P/F 31.20.612.7023
E-MAIL ceo@corporateeurope.org
www.corporateeurope.org

European-based research and campaign group targeting the threats to democracy, equity, social justice and the environment posed by the economic and political power of corporations and their lobby groups.

Focus on the Global South (FOCUS)
c/o CUSRI,
Wisit Prachuabmoh Building
Chulalongkorn University
Bangkok 10330, Thailand
P 66.2.218.7363
F 66.2.255.9976
E-MAIL admin@focusweb.org
www.focusweb.org

Progressive development policy research and practice, dedicated to regional and global policy analysis, micro-macro linking and advocacy work. FOCUS works with NGOs and people's organizations in the Asian Pacific and other regions.

Program on Corporations, Law and Democracy (POCLAD)
PO Box 246
South Yarmouth, MA 02664
P 509.398.1145
F 509.398.1552
E-MAIL people@poclad.org
www.poclad.org

"Contesting the authority of corporations to govern." POCLAD provides useful critiques of the limitations of attacking the symptoms of corporate power, and suggests ways to redefine rather than regulate corporations.

United for a Fair Economy
37 Temple Place, 2nd Floor
Boston, MA 02111
P 617.423.2148
F 617.423.0191
www.ufenet.org

Exposes the dangers of growing income, wage and wealth inequality in the United States and coordinates action to reduce the gap, provides popular education resources, works with grassroots organizations, conducts research, and supports creative and legislative action to reduce inequality.

ENDNOTES \ REFERENCES CITED

[1] William Greider, *One World, Ready or Not: The Manic Logic of Global Capitalism* (Touchstone, 1997), p. 24-25.

[2] The largest corporations are ranked by business publications such as *Fortune, Forbes* and *Business Week.* The social and environmental impacts of those corporations are monitored by Corporate Watch, http://www.corpwatch.org, Corporate Europe Observatory, http://www.corporateeurope.org, Project Underground, http://www.moles.org, and other public interest organizations. See also George Draffan, *Directory of Transnational Corporations,* http://www.endgame.org.

[3] Philip Burch, *The Managerial Revolution Reassessed* (Heath, 1972). Michael Schwartz, editor, *The Structure of Power in America: The Corporate Elite as a Ruling Class* (Holmes & Meier, 1987), p. 7ff.

[4] G. William Domhoff, *Who Rules America?: Power and Politics in the Year 2000* (Mayfield, 1998), p. 144, citing Val Burris, Elite Policy Planning Networks in the United States, *Research in Politics and Sociology,* 1992, 4: 126.

[5] Herbert I. Schiller, *Culture, Inc.: The Corporate Takeover of Public Expression* (Oxford University Press, 1991). Richard Howard Robbins, *Global Problems and the Culture of Capitalism* (Allyn & Bacon, 1998).

[6] John Gaventa, *Power and Powerlessness: Quiescence and Rebellion in an Appalachian Valley.* (University of Illinois Press, 1980). Antonio Gramsci, State and Civil Society, in *Selections from the Prison Notebooks* (Lawrence and Wishart, 1971). Paulo Freire, *The Pedagogy of the Oppressed.* (Penguin, 1972). Ralph Miliband, *The State in Capitalist Society: An Analysis of the Western Systems of Power* (Weidenfeld and Nicolson, 1969).

[7] Charles Lewis, Media Money: How Corporate Spending Blocked Political Ad Reform, *Columbia Journalism Review,* Sept-Oct 2000.

[8] Fairness & Accuracy in Reporting, Action Alert: The Commercialization of Children's Public Television, March 15, 2000, http://www.fair.org. *See also* James Ledbetter, *Made Possible By: The Death of Public Broadcasting in the United States* (Verso).

[9] Thomas C. Frank, Liberation Marketing and the Culture Trust, excerpted from *Conglomerates and the Media* (New Press, 1997) in *The Sun,* March 1999. Those who like to consume books would do well to read Toby M. Smith, *The Myth of Green Marketing: Tending Our Goats at the Edge of Apocalypse* (University of Toronto Press, 1998). Roger Rosenblatt, et al., editors, *Consuming Desires: Consumption, Culture, and the Pursuit of Happiness* (Shearwater Books, 1999). Juliet Schor and Douglas B. Holt, editors, *The Consumer Society Reader* (New Press, 2000). Gary Cross, *An All-Consuming Century: Why Commercialism Won in Modern America* (Columbia University Press, 2000).

[10] Hoover's Online Advertising Industry Snapshot, http://www.hoovers.com.

[11] Council of Public Relations Firms, 1999 Public Relations Industry Rankings, http://www.prfirms.org/InfoCenter/1999factsheet.html, August 23, 2000.

[12] Thomas L. Harris/Impulse Research, 1999 Public Relations Client Survey, http://www.cyberpulse.com/harris/index.html, August 23, 2000.

13 Hoover's Online capsule,
http://www.hoovers.com/co/capsule/0/0,2163,43120,00.html.

14 Geoffry D. White et al., editors, *Campus, Inc: Corporate Power in the Ivory Tower* (Prometheus, 2000). Lawrence C. Soley, *Leasing the Ivory Tower: The Corporate Takeover of Academia* (South End Press, 1995). *See also* the website of the Center for the Analysis of Commercialism in Education,
http://www.uwm.edu/Dept/CACE/.

15 Lawrence C. Soley, *Leasing the Ivory Tower: The Corporate Takeover of Academia* (South End Press, 1995).

16 Rebecca S. Lowen, *Creating the Cold War University: The Transformation of Stanford* (University of California Press, 1997).

17 Max B. Sawicky and Alex Molnar, *The Hidden Costs of Channel One: Estimates for the Fifty States,* April 1998,
http://www.uwm.edu/Dept/CACE/documents/hidden_costs2.html.

18 Hoover's Online, http://www.hoovers.com/capsules/40258.html.

19 Alex Molnar and Jennifer Morales, Commercialism@School.com (Center for the Analysis of Commercialism in Education, September 2000),
http://www.uwm.edu/Dept/CACE/documents/cace-00-02.htm.

20 Sally Covington, *Moving a Public Policy Agenda: The Strategic Philanthropy of Conservative Foundations* (National Committee for Responsive Philanthropy, 1997) and *Conservative Foundations Prevail in Shaping Public Policies: New Report Documents Public Policy Impact of 12 Core Foundations,*
http://ncrp.org/psr/pressreleases/conservative.htm. *See also* Christopher Georges, Conservative Heritage Foundation Finds Recipe for Influence, *Wall Street Journal,* Aug. 10, 1995, p. A10; and Russ Bellant, *The Coors Connection: How Coors Family Philanthropy Undermines Democratic Pluralism* (South End Press, 1991). Right-wing foundations and front-groups are tracked by several organizations, including Public Research Associates and Western States Center. Corporate foundation funding of liberal organizations is tracked by Capital Research Center http://www.capitalresearch.org.

21 National Education Association, The State-Based Assault,
http://www.nea.org/publiced/paycheck/paychkg.html.

22 Charles William Maynes, A Closing Word, *Foreign Policy,* March 1, 1997.

23 Quote is from Maynes, *Foreign Policy,* March 1, 1997. Comment about Heritage is from Georges, *Wall Street Journal,* Aug. 10, 1995, p. A10.

24 Through pamphlets and articles and "rethinking the corporation" conversations, the Program on Corporations, Law and Democracy is reminding activists of their populist history and redirecting energy into direct challenging of corporate power. See http://www.poclad.org and Appendix 8 for contact information.

25 Michael Useem, *The Inner Circle: Large Corporations and the Rise of Business Political Activity in the U.S. and U.K.* (Oxford University Press, 1984), p. 77.

26 The Committee for Economic Development (CED) has been called the domestic offshoot of the CFR. CED's trustees are representative of the major U.S. corporations. CED has offices in New York and Washington DC; its website is at http://www.ced.org.

27 G. William Domhoff, *Who Rules America?: Power and Politics in the Year 2000* (Mayfield, 1998), p. 263, citing Thomas R. Wolanin, *Presidential Advisory*

Commissions (University of Wisconsin, 1975). The CED was a study group founded (and funded) by corporate leaders during World War II to help plan the postwar economy. The CED helped convince conservatives of the usefulness of the World Bank and International Monetary Fund. For the history and internal politics of the CED, see Domhoff, p. 150-155.

28 Ann Crittenden, Aide Reflects Schultz Style, *New York Times*, July 21, 1982, p. D1.

29 A good case study of extensive political connections is Laton McCartney's *Friends in High Places: The Bechtel Story: The Most Secret Corporation and How It Engineered the World* (Simon and Schuster, 1988).

30 G. William Domhoff, *Who Rules America?: Power and Politics in the Year 2000* (Mayfield, 1998), p. 251-255.

31 Domhoff, p. 249, citing Beth Mintz, The President's Cabinet, 1897-1972, *Insurgent Sociologist*, Spring 1975; and Philip Burch, *Elites in American History* (Holmes & Meier, 1980-1981).

32 David Vogel, *Fluctuating Fortunes: The Political Power of Business in America* (Basic Books, 1989), p. 195, 197-198.

33 Council of Public Relations Firms, 1999 Public Relations Industry Rankings, http://www.prfirms.org/InfoCenter/1999factsheet.html, August 23, 2000.

34 Charles Lewis and the Center for Public Integrity, *The Buying of the President 2000*, (Avon, 2000), p. 5. James Heintz et al., *The Ultimate Field Guide to the U.S. Economy* (New Press, 2000), p. 98.

35 Center for Responsive Politics, http://www.opensecrets.org/pubs/lobby98/totsector.htm.

36 The expenditures and clients of lobbying firms are public information filed with the U.S. Federal Election Commission; the Center for Responsive Politics has a user-friendly website for tracking lobbying expenditures at http://www.opensecrets.org.

37 Center for Responsive Politics, http://opensecrets.org/pubs/lobby98/totsector.htm.

38 Charles Lewis and the Center for Public Integrity, *The Buying of the President 2000* (Avon, 2000), p. 22.

39 G. William Domhoff, *Who Rules America?: Power and Politics in the Year 2000* (Mayfield, 1998), p. 241.

40 Common Cause, Ten Most Expensive Senate Races, http://commoncause.org/publications/110698_chart2.html and Center for Responsive Politics, http://www.opensecrets.org/home/index.htm, August 30, 2000.

41 Common Cause, The Influence of PACs, http://www.commoncause.org/pressroom/congress_pacs.html.

42 Common Cause, Party Contributions & Soft Money, http://www.commoncause.org/pressroom/congress_contributions.html. and http://commoncause.org/publications/july00/072500.htm and http://www.commoncause.org/soft_money/study99/chart7.html.

43 "Double giver" data is tracked at the Common Cause website http://www.commoncause.org/soft_money/study99/chart7.html.

44 Common Cause, http://www.commoncause.org/issue_agenda/glossary.htm#4.

45 Amy Rinard, Cities, Towns Step Up Their Legislative Lobbying, *Milwaukee Journal*, Aug. 21, 2000.

[46] U.S. House Committee on Natural Resources, Subcommittee on Oversight and Investigations, *Taking from the Taxpayer: Public Subsidies for Natural Resource Development.* 103d Cong., 2d Sess., Committee print No. 8, August 1994.

[47] A breakdown of Estes' externalities is available in his book *Tyranny of the Bottom Line: Why Corporations Make Good People Do Bad Things* (Barret-Koehler, 1996). An abbreviated version is available on the Internet at http://www.endgame.org/endgame.html.

[48] David Korten, *The Post-Corporate World: Life After Capitalism* (Kumarian Press and Berrett-Koehler, 1999), p. 48.

[49] There were 85,064 corporate mergers valued at $3.5 trillion during the Reagan-Bush years (1980-1992), and 166,310 corporate mergers valued at $9.8 trillion during the Clinton Years (1992-1999), according to the Securities Data Company, cited in Agribusiness Examiner, #89, Oct 4, 2000, http://www.ea1.com/CARP/. *Mergerstat Review,* available in business libraries, tracks corporate mergers.

[50] For the history and geopolitics of petroleum, see Anthony Sampson, *The Seven Sisters;* and Daniel Yergin, *The Prize: The Epic Quest for Oil, Money, and Power* (Simon & Schuster, 1991).

[51] The dominant corporations in various industries are listed at http://www.endgame.org/oligopolies.html.

[52] Lori Wallach and Michelle Sforza, *Whose Trade Organization? Corporate Globalization and the Erosion of Democracy* (Public Citizen, 1999).

[53] Steve Brouwer, *Sharing the Pie: A Citizen's Guide to Wealth and Power in America* (Henry Holt, 1998), p. 59, 72.

[54] Walter Adams and James Brock explored the limits to growth in their book *The Bigness Complex: Industry, Labor, and Government in the American Economy* (Pantheon, 1986), and showed how corporate mergers are unproductive in *Dangerous Pursuits: Mergers and Acquisitions in the Age of Wall Street* (Pantheon, 1989).

[55] OPIC 1991 Annual Report, p. 30; and Alan C. Brennglass, *The Overseas Private Investment Corporation: A Study in Political Risk* (Praeger, 1983), p. 219-220.

[56] Brennglass, p. 120ff.

[57] Brennglass, p.124.

[58] Brennglass, p. 70ff, 128-129.

[59] A list of public institution shareholders is at http://www.endgame.org/shareholder-contacts.html.

[60] Data from U.S. House Committee to Investigate Concentration of Control of Money and Credit, 1913: 56-91; and from Willard F. Mueller, *A Primer on Monopoly and Competition* (Random House, 1970), p. 42.

[61] Quote from Chalmers Johnson, *Blowback: The Costs and Consequences of American Empire* (Metropolitan, 2000), p. 201. *See also* Joel Kurtzman, *The Death of Money: How the Electronic Economy Has Destabilized the World's Markets and Created Financial Chaos* (Simon & Schuster, 1993).

[62] Mark Weisbrot, Globalization for Whom?, *Cornell International Law Journal,* 1998 Symposium Issue, Vol. 31, No. 3.

[63] Loan guarantees come in various forms, but often a loan is made to a developing country "to allow that country to be able to pay for an export contract. It will

usually be made by the exporting company or a commercial bank. Part or all of the scheduled repayments are then guaranteed against the risk of non-payment by the government of the exporting country. These guarantees are issued by the national export credit agency, which will also supply insurance against political risk." (ECA-Watch, Introduction to Export Credit Agencies: Creating Risk, Generating Debt and Guaranteeing Environmental Destruction, http://www.eca-watch.org/introduction.html).

[64] ECA-Watch has a list and links to the major export credit agencies at http://www.eca-watch.org/ecas.html.

[65] ECA-Watch, Introduction to Export Credit Agencies: Creating Risk, Generating Debt and Guaranteeing Environmental Destruction, http://www.eca-watch.org/introduction.html.

[66] Michiel Van Voorst/Eurodad, Debt Creating Aspects of Export Credits, August 1998, http://www.eca-watch.org/debtecas.html.

[67] For good introductions to the mechanisms and impacts of structural adjustment, see Walden Bello with Shea Cunningham and Bill Rau, *Dark Victory: The United States, Structural Adjustment and Global Poverty* (Food First, 1994, revised 1999) and Michel Chossudovsky, *The Globalisation of Poverty: Impacts of IMF and World Bank Reforms* (Third World Network, 1997). Chossudovsky's case studies of structural adjustment in Somalia, Rwanda, India, Bangladesh, Vietnam, Brazil, Peru, Bolivia, Russia and Yugoslavia help explain much of the unrest and crisis in those countries.

[68] The latest statistics on health and income can be found in the various annual reports of the World Bank, the UN Development Program (UNDP), and the UN Commission on Trade and Development (UNCTAD), which are available in libraries and from the agencies' websites.

[69] Data is from OECD, *Financial Market Trends,* No. 66, 1997. A recent discussion of the impacts and resistance is Thomas W. Collins and John D. Wingard, editors, *Communities and Capital: Local Struggles Against Corporate Power and Privatization* (University of Georgia Press, 2000).

[70] The methods and impacts of the trade agreements are documented in Lori Wallach and Michelle Sforza, *Whose Trade Organization? Corporate Globalization and the Erosion of Democracy* (Public Citizen, 1999).

[71] The bribery and politics behind the North American Free Trade Agreement are described by John R. MacArthur, *The Selling of "Free Trade": NAFTA, Washington, and the Subversion of American Democracy* (Hill And Wang, 2000).

[72] MacArthur, p. 221.

[73] The history of police and National Guard violence against striking workers is told by Jeremy Brecher, *Strike!* (South End Press, 1972, revised 1997).

[74] The International Confederation of Free Trade Unions publishes an Annual Survey of Violations of Trade Union Rights at its website, http://www.icftu.org, and LaborNet and its international affiliates monitor labor organizing in many countries, http://www.labornet.org/.

[75] Daniel Burton-Rose, Dan Pens, and Paul Wright, editors, *The Celling of America: An Inside Look at the Prison Industry* (Common Courage Press, 1998).

[76] Jisuk Woo and Jeffrey D. Kentor, *Capital and Coercion : The Economic and Military Processes That Have Shaped the World Economy, 1800-1990* (Garland

Publishing, 2000). Charles Lipson, *Standing Guard: Protecting Foreign Capital in the Nineteenth and Twentieth Centuries* (University of California Press, 1985).

[77] Lipson, p. 13-16.

[78] Jonathan D. Spence, *The Search for Modern China* (W.W. Norton, 1990), p. 152-164.

[79] U.S. corporate influence in Guatemala did not end, of course. In 1975, the head of United Fruit committed suicide, as his million-dollar bribe to the Honduran Economic Minster (to obtain a reduction in the Honduran export tax on bananas) became known. Two weeks later, the Honduran government fell. Investigations by the U.S. Congress and Securities & Exchange Commission uncovered bribery by more than 350 U.S. corporations (Brennglass, 1983, p.159-160).

[80] Michael Klare, *Resource Wars: Global Geopolitics in the 21st Century* (Metropolitan Books, 2001).

[81] T.J. Figueroa, Behind the Outcry over War Diamonds: Washington, London Intervene in Sierra Leone, Seek Greater Influence in Africa, *The Militant,* Aug 28, 2000, http://www.themilitant.com/2000/6433/643310.html; Sierra Leone: A Brutal War For Diamonds, *Workers Power Global,* June 8, 2000, http://www.workerspower.com/wpglobal/sierraleonejune2k.html.

[82] Daniel Yergin, *The Prize: The Epic Quest for Oil, Money, and Power* (Simon & Schuster, 1991).

[83] Human Rights Watch, *Colombia: Human Rights Concerns Raised By The Security Arrangements Of Transnational Oil Companies,* April 1998, http://www.igc.org/hrw/advocacy/corporations/colombia/Oilpat.htm.

[84] Michael T. Klare, The Real Reason for U.S. Aid to Colombia, *MoJo Wire,* April 7, 2000, http://www.motherjones.com/news_wire/colombia.html; and also his article Quest for Oil Drives Aid to Colombia, *AlterNet,* May 4, 2000, http://www.angelfire.com/mn/cispes/colo5400.html, citing *Newsweek,* April 3, 2000.

[85] James Robbins, Wagons East: International Trade and the FRY-NATO War, Academy for Peace, http://www.zoran.net/afp/text/submitted/wagons_east.htm. Stuart Parrott, Pipeline Superhighway Replaces The Silk Road, London, Nov 19 1997.

[86] Ken Silverstein, Privatizing War, *The Nation,* July 28, 1997, p. 11-17.

[87] William Blum's *Killing Hope: U.S. Military and CIA Intervention Since World War II* is a comprehensive view of U.S. military actions around the world.

[88] Steve Brouwer, *Sharing the Pie: A Citizen's Guide to Wealth and Power in America* (Henry Holt, 1998), p. 90.

[89] Chalmers Johnson, *Blowback: The Costs and Consequences of American Empire* (Metropolitan, 2000), p. 87. *See also* John Tirman, *Spoils of War: The Human Cost of America's Arms Trade* (Free Press, 1997).

[90] Chalmers Johnson, *Blowback: The Costs and Consequences of American Empire* (Metropolitan, 2000), p. 87.

[91] James Heintz et al., *The Ultimate Field Guide to the U.S. Economy* (New Press, 2000), p. 99.

[92] William D. Hartung, *The Costs of NATO Expansion Revisited: From the Costs of*

Modernization to the Costs of War, World Policy Institute Issue Brief, Arms Trade Resource Center, April 21, 1999.

[93] The Program on Corporations, Law and Democracy is providing a useful critique of the limitations of attacking the symptoms of corporate power; *see address in Appendix 8.*

[94] AEI 1999 Annual Report, http://www.aei.org/annual/finances.htm.

[95] AEI 1999 Annual Report, http://www.aei.org/annual/trustee.htm.

[96] AEI 1999 Annual Report, http://www.aei.org/annual/finances.htm.

[97] http://www.aei.org/research/description.htm#2.

[98] AEI 1999 Annual Report, http://www.aei.org/annual/foreign4.htm.

[99] Bilderberg news release, May 14, 1998.

[100] *Congressional Record,* Volume 110, Part 6, April 11, 1964, p. 7684-7685.

[101] Quoted at http://whiterabbitcult.com/Bilderberg/Bilderberg.html.

[102] According to a list compiled by Grattan Healy, http://ourworld.compuserve.com/homepages/grattan_healy/Bild-az-tab.html.

[103] Bilderberg press release, June 3, 2000.

[104] Brookings Institution website, http://www.brookings.org, *Encyclopedia of Interest Groups and Lobbyists in the United States* (Gale, 2000), p. 472-474. Donald Critchlow, *The Brookings Institution, 1916-1952* (Northern Illinois University Press, 1985). Charles Saunders, *The Brookings Institution: A Fifty-Year History* (Brookings).

[105] David Vogel, *Fluctuating Fortunes: The Political Power of Business in America* (Basic Books, 1989).

[106] Laton McCartney, *Friends in High Places: The Bechtel Story: The Most Secret Corporation and How It Engineered the World* (Simon and Schuster, 1988), p. 106.

[107] *Encyclopedia of Associations* (Gale Research, 1996).

[108] Business Roundtable, http://www.brtable.org/about.cfm/introduction, March 6, 2000.

[109] *Encyclopedia of Interest Groups and Lobbyists in the United States* (Sharpe, 2000), p. 318-320. For lobbying expenses see Center for Responsive Politics, http://www.opensecrets.org/pubs/lobby98/topspend.htm.

[110] Business Roundtable, http://www.brtable.org/about.cfm/introduction, January 23, 2000.

[111] John R. MacArthur, *The Selling of "Free Trade": NAFTA, Washington, and the Subversion of American Democracy* (Hill And Wang, 2000), p. 222, 227, 271. MacArthur cites a June 1997 Business Roundtable news release and a July 1997 White House "Study on the Operation and Effect of the NAFTA."

[112] Rick Anderson, Some Call It Bribery: Did Condit Make an Offer Congress Can't Refuse? *Seattle Weekly,* Feb. 24, 2000, p. 16.

[113] Michael R. Bonsignore, Testimony on behalf of the U.S.-China Business Council and the Business Roundtable, On the U.S.-China Bilateral Trade Agreement and the Accession of China to the WTO, before the U.S. House Ways & Means Committee, February 16th, 2000.

[114] Business Roundtable, http://www.brtable.org/about.cfm/officers, January 23, 2000.

115 G. William Domhoff, *Who Rules America?: Power and Politics in the Year 2000* (Mayfield, 1998), p. 158.

116 Business Roundtable, http://www.brtable.org/taskforces.cfm, January 23, 2000.

117 Cato website, www.cato.org. The Cato Institute operates many other websites as well, including www.socialsecurity.org, www.freetrade.org, www.libertarianism.org, www.individualrights.org, www.elcato.org, www.cato-university.org.

118 Three family foundations operated by the Kochs (the Charles G. Koch, David H. Koch and Claude R. Lambe Charitable Foundations) were instrumental in creating the Cato Institute and Citizens for a Sound Economy; between 1986 and 1990, Koch money to these two groups totaled $6.5 million and $4.8 million, respectively (People for the American Way, *Buying A Movement: Right-Wing Foundations and American Politics*, http://www.pfaw.org/issues/right/rw/rep_rwfound.html).

119 http://www.cato.org/research/reglt-st.html.

120 Stephen Moore and Dean Stansel, *Ending Corporate Welfare As We Know It*, Cato Institute Policy Analysis No. 225, May 12, 1995, http://cato.org/pa225.html. James Bovard, *Archer Daniels Midland: A Case Study in Corporate Welfare*, Cato Institute Policy Analysis No. 241, Sept 26, 1995, http://www.cato.rg/pa241.html.

121 http://www.cato.org/research/mon-st.html.

122 http://www.cato.org/research/glob-st.html.

123 Dan Morgan, Think Tanks: Corporations' Quiet Weapon, *Washington Post*, Jan 29, 2000, p. A1.

124 Karen Charman, Saving the Planet With Pestilent Statistics, *PR Watch*, Fourth Quarter 1999, http://www.prwatch.org/prw_issues/1999-Q4/index.html.

125 Cheney pointed to sanctions against Iran, which prevented U.S. oil companies such as his own from getting access to lucrative oil deposits. Richard Cheney, Defending Liberty in a Global Economy, speech delivered at Cato Institute's *Collateral Damage Conference*, June 23, 1998.

126 http://www.cato.org/about/about.html.

127 http://www.cato.org/about/about.html.

128 *Encyclopedia of Interest Groups and Lobbyists in the United States* (Sharpe, 2000), p. 475-476.

129 http://www.cato.org/events/calendar.html.

130 http://www.cse.org/know/mission.html.

131 Funding data compiled from the John M. Olin Foundation website, http://www.jmof.org/grants/; the Scaife Foundations website, http://www.scaife.com; from Dan Morgan, Think Tanks: Corporations' Quiet Weapon, *Washington Post*, Jan 29, 2000, p. A1; and from People for the American Way, *Buying A Movement: Right-Wing Foundations and American Politics*, http://www.pfaw.org/issues/right/rw/rep_rwfound.html.

132 Conference Board website, www.conference-board.org, Feb. 2000.

133 Quotes are from the Conference Board website, http://www.conference-board.org/whoweare/frames.cfm?main=about.cfm, March 6, 2000, and from Joseph L. Naar, *An Historical Celebration of The*

Conference Board's 75th Anniversary (Conference Board, 1991), p. 1.

134 Naar, p. 13.

135 Naar, p. 36, 38.

136 Tony Gosling, PEPIS #17, Feb 28, 2000.

137 Joseph L. Naar, *An Historical Celebration* (Conference Board, 1991), p. 38.

138 Naar, p. 25-26.

139 Naar, p. 39.

140 Naar, p. 39.

141 Naar, p. 41.

142 Conference Board, http://www.conference-board.org/, March 6, 2000.

143 Conference Board,
http://www.conference-board.org/whoweare/frames.cfm?main=about.cfm,
March 6, 2000.

144 As of March 2000.

145 Joseph L. Naar, *An Historical Celebration* (Conference Board, 1991), p. 39.

146 Naar, p. 43.

147 http://www.ert.be/pe/ene_frame.htm, August 1, 2000.

148 Russell Mokhiber and Robert Weissman, The Billionaire Mindset and Wealth
Inequality, *Focus on the Corporation*, Aug 16, 2000,
http://www.corporatepredators.org.

149 Conference Board,
http://www.conference-board.org/whoweare/frames.cfm?main=about.cfm,
March 6, 2000.

150 Conference Board,
http://www.conference-board.org/whoweare/frames.cfm?main=about.cfm,
March 6, 2000.

151 Conference Board,
http://www.conference-board.org/whoweare/frames.cfm?main=about.cfm,
March 6, 2000.

152 Council on Foreign Relations, http://www.foreignrelations.org/public/about.html,
January 23, 2000.

153 Council on Foreign Relations,
http://www.foreignrelations.org/public/bd.html, January 23, 2000.

154 http://www.cfr.org/public/ms.html, June 14, 2000.

155 This history relies on Laurence H. Shoup and William Minter, *Imperial Brain
Trust: The Council on Foreign Relations and United States Foreign Policy*
(Monthly Review Press, 1977).

156 CFR website, http://www.foreignrelations.org/public/about.html and
http://www.cfr.org/public/mi.html.

157 http://www.cfr.org/public/ms.html, June 14, 2000.

158 NPR, Talk Of The Nation, September 4, 1996.

159 Raymond Vernon, editor, *The Promise of Privatization: A Challenge for
American Foreign Policy* (Council on Foreign Relations, 1988), p. 7.

160 CFR website, http://www.cfr.org/public/special.html#taskforces.

[161] My profile of the ERT relies heavily on Belen Balanya et al., *Europe Inc.: Regional & Global Restructuring and the Rise of Corporate Power* (Pluto Press, 2000). The quote from ERT is from its webpage, http://www.ert.be/pc/enc_frame.htm, August 1, 2000.

[162] Belen Balanya et al., *Europe Inc.: Regional & Global Restructuring and the Rise of Corporate Power* (Pluto Press, 2000), p. 21-31.

[163] http://www.ert.be/pg/eng_frame.htm, August 1, 2000.

[164] Belen Balanya et al., *Europe Inc.: Regional & Global Restructuring and the Rise of Corporate Power* (Pluto Press, 2000), p. 29-30.

[165] See Chapter 8 of Balanya, *Europe Inc.* for discussion of the politics of expanding European infrastructure.

[166] Tabaksblat is also vice chair of the Conference Board (USA), and a member of the Supervisory Boards of AEGON NV, TNT Post Group NV, and VEBA AG, as well as chairman of the board of governors of Leiden University Medical Centre and chairman of the Mauritshuis Museum in The Hague.

[167] http://www.ert.be/pc/enc_frame.htm, August 1, 2000.

[168] http://www.ert.be/pd/end_frame.htm, August 1, 2000.

[169] Belen Balanya et al., *Europe Inc.: Regional & Global Restructuring and the Rise of Corporate Power* (Pluto Press, 2000), p. 33-36.

[170] ERT chairman Morris Tabaksblat, speech at European Business Summit, June 10, 2000, http://www.ert.be/pe/ene_frame.htm, August 1, 2000.

[171] Carl Deal, *The Greenpeace Guide to Anti-Environmental Organizations* (Odonian Press, 1993), p. 57-59.

[172] Testimony before the U.S. Subcommittee on National Security, Veterans Affairs, and International Relations, Sept 8, 2000.

[173] http://www.heritage.org/library/categories/budgettax/bg1058.html.

[174] http://www.heritage.org/library/execmemo/em625.html.

[175] http://www.heritage.org/library/categories/govern/bg1094.html.

[176] *Encyclopedia of Interest Groups and Lobbyists in the United States* (Sharpe, 2000).

[177] http://www.hoover.org/develop/brochure/programmatic.html.

[178] http://www.hoover.org/develop/brochure/testimony.html.

[179] http://www-hoover.org/develop/brochure/media.html.

[180] http://www-hoover.org/PubAffairs/ar98/commun.html.

[181] http://www-hoover.org/PubAffairs/ar98/commun.html.

[182] http://www-hoover.org/PubAffairs/ar98/commun.html.

[183] G. William Domhoff, *Who Rules America?: Power and Politics in the Year 2000* (Mayfield, 1998), p. 142-143.

[184] Hoover Institution, 1998 Annual Report.

[185] http://www.hoover.org/develop/brochure/resources.html and http://www-hoover.org/develop/brochure/funding.html. See also James M. Barrett, The Federal Government and the Powers Behind It, September 13, 1999, Milwaukee Pledge of Resistance Foreign Policy Watchdog website, http://www.execpc.com/~forpolcy/Frpolply.html

[186] Hoover Institution, 1998 Annual Report.

[187] Karen Charman, Saving the Planet With Pestilent Statistics, PR *Watch,* Fourth Quarter 1999, http://www.prwatch.org/prw_issues/1999-Q4/index.html.

[188] *Encyclopedia of Interest Groups and Lobbyists in the United States* (Sharpe, 2000), p. 492-493.

[189] Unless otherwise noted, the direct quotes in this profile are from ICC's website, http://www.iccwbo.org/.

[190] *Europa Directory of International Organizations* (Europa Publications, 1999), p. 341ff.

[191] http://www.iccwbo.org/home/intro_icc/leadership.asp.

[192] http://www.iccwbo.org/home/conferences/budapest/index.asp.

[193] *Europa Directory of International Organizations,* p. 378-384.

[194] For a summary and chronology of events, see George Draffan, Oil Wars: The Balkans, http://www.endgame.org/oilwars-balkans.html. For analysis of the strategic and economic issues, see Assembly of the Western European Union, Document 1586, The Situation in Central Asia and the Caucasus and European Security, November 19, 1997, http://assembly.weu.int/eng/reports/1586-2.html. For one of the better journalistic accounts, see Frank Viviano, Caspian Ring of Fire: Raging War Zones Surround Planned Network of Oil Export Pipelines, *San Francisco Chronicle,* August 11, 1998, p. A1. For coverage of the lobbying and interlocks, see Christopher Hitchens, When It Comes to the Great Game of Influence, Bill Clinton Knows How to Play by the Rules, *Salon,* Sept 29, 1997, http://www.salon.com/sept97/columnists/hitchens970929.html and David Ottaway and Dan Morgan, Former Top U.S. Aides Seek Caspian Gusher, *Washington Post,* July 6, 1997.

[195] The top five countries listed accounted for 91 percent of the total. Stockholm International Peace Research Institute, http://projects.sipri.se/milex_major_spenders.html and http://projects.sipri.se/arms-strade/at1.pdf.

[196] William D. Hartung, *Welfare for Weapons Dealers 1998,* World Policy Institute Issue Brief, March 1998, http://worldpolicy.org/projects/arms/reports.html.

[197] The Commerce Department's market analyses have included the June 1995 *European Diversification and Defense Market Assessment* and the October 1997 *National Export Strategy.*

[198] William D. Hartung, *Welfare for Weapons Dealers 1998,* World Policy Institute Issue Brief, March 1998, http://worldpolicy.org/projects/arms/reports.html.

[199] *Europa Directory of International Organizations,* p. 378-384.

[200] William D. Hartung, *The Costs of NATO Expansion Revisited,* World Policy Institute Issue Brief, APRIL 21, 1999, http://worldpolicy.org/projects/arms/reports.html.

[201] William D. Hartung, *Welfare for Weapons Dealers 1998,* World Policy Institute Issue Brief, March 1998 and *The Costs of NATO Expansion Revisited,* World Policy Institute Issue Brief, April 21, 1999, both at http://worldpolicy.org/projects/arms/reports.html.

[202] William D. Hartung, *The Costs of NATO Expansion Revisited,* World Policy Institute Issue Brief, April 21, 1999, http://worldpolicy.org/projects/arms/reports.html.

203 The lobbying and campaign contributions of various industries are ranked by the Center for Responsive Politics, http//www.opensecrets.org/pubs/lobby98/totsector.htm.

204 William D. Hartung, *Welfare for Weapons Dealers 1998*, World Policy Institute Issue Brief, March 1998, http://worldpolicy.org/projects/arms/reports.html.

205 William D. Hartung, *Welfare for Weapons Dealers 1998*, World Policy Institute Issue Brief, March 1998, http://worldpolicy.org/projects/arms/reports.html.

206 William D. Hartung, *Welfare for Weapons Dealers 1998*, World Policy Institute Issue Brief, March 1998, http://worldpolicy.org/projects/arms/reports.html.

207 William D. Hartung, *Welfare for Weapons Dealers 1998*, World Policy Institute Issue Brief, March 1998, http://worldpolicy.org/projects/arms/reports.html.

208 http://www.rand.org/50TH/.

209 http://www.rand.org/ABOUT/index.html.

210 http://www.rand.org/50TH/.

211 http://www.rand.org/50TH/,

212 From an interview published in the *Detroit News*.

213 http://www.rand.org/organization/paf/about.html.

214 http://www.rand.org/natsec/secenvironav.html.

215 http://www.rand.org/publications/MR/.

216 http://www.rand.org/natsec/nsrd/intel.html and http://www.rand.org/natsec/prodnav.html.

217 http://www.rand.org/natsec/nsrd/allied.html.

218 *O'Dwyer's Washington Report*, Feb 7, 2000, http://www.odwyerpr.com/washrpt/washo207.htm.

219 http://www.rand.org/publications/MR/MR994/MR994.pdf.

220 Charles Swett, Strategic Assessment: The Internet (July 1995), http://www.fas.org/cp/swett.html. *See also* Jason Wehling, Netwars and Activists' Power on the Internet, March 1995, http://www.spunk.org/library/comms/spoo1518/Netwars.html as well as the discussion at http://gopher.well.sf.ca.us:70/0/Military/cyberwar.

221 Selina Jackson, The TABD Process: A Business Approach to US-EU Trade Policy, *EABC Official Journal*, Spring 1998, http://tabd.com.

222 Belen Balanya et al., *Europe Inc.: Regional & Global Restructuring and the Rise of Corporate Power* (Pluto Press, 2000), p. 104.

223 Corporate Europe Observatory, Transatlantic Business Dialogue (TABD): Putting the Business Horse Before the Government Cart, *Corporate Europe Observatory Briefing Paper*, 25 October 1999, http://www.corporateeurope.org/tabd/berlinbriefing.html.

224 Transatlantic Business Dialogue, http://www.tabd.com/index1.html, January 23, 2000. The TABD's 1995 Seville report declared its "full support for the rules and principles of the World Trade Organization (WTO) and other relevant institutions, and the need to ensure any bilateral or plurilateral agreements are WTO compatible."

225 TABD news release, February 17, 2000, http://tabd.com.

226 Holly Sklar, The Commission's Purpose, Structure, and Programs—In Its Own

Words, in *Trilateralism: The Trilateral Commission and Elite Planning for World Management* (South End Press, 1980), p. 83-84.

[227] Trilateral Commission, http://www.trilateral.org/memb.htm, January 23, 2000.

[228] Trilateral Commission, http://www.trilateral.org/annmtgs/annmtgs.htm.

[229] Trilateral Commission, http://www.trilateral.org/memb.htm, January 23, 2000.

[230] Trilateral Commission, http://www.trilateral.org/annmtgs/annmtgs.htm.

[231] The meeting agendas are at http://www.trilateral.org/annmtgs/programs/anmplist.htm and transcripts of talks are at http://www.trilateral.org/annmtgs/trialog/trlgtxts/t53/t53.htm.

[232] Holly Sklar, The Commission's Purpose, Structure, and Programs: In Its Own Words, in *Trilateralism: The Trilateral Commission and Elite Planning for World Management* (South End Press, 1980), p. 86.

[233] UNICE website, http://www.unice.org.

[234] *Corporate Europe Observer,* Issue 5, October 1999, The Global Compact: The UN's New Deal with Global Corporate Citizens. *See also* Corporate Europe Observatory's *The Corporate Co-Optation of the UN.*

[235] *Europa Directory of International Organizations,* p. 85-86.

[236] *Europa Directory of International Organizations,* p. 87-90.

[237] http://www.undp.org/hdro/99.htm.

[238] Cited in *Corporate Europe Observer,* Issue 5, October 1999. Annan has been with the United Nations system since 1962, holding positions with the World Health Organization, the High Commissioner for Human Rights in Geneva, the UN Economic Commission for Africa, and serving as head of the UN Peacekeeping Department from 1993-1996. He was appointed United Nations secretary-general in 1997.

[239] Quotes are from a speech at the Geneva 2000 Forum on the eve of the Social Summit, quoted by Nicola Bullard, Focus on the Global South, *Focus On Trade,* Number 52, August 2000, http://www.focusweb and from an address to the United States Chamber of Commerce, in Washington, D.C., June 8, 1999, UN Press Release SG/SM/7022.

[240] *Corporate Europe Observer,* Issue 5, October 1999.

[241] Secretary-General Proposes Global Compact on Human Rights, Labour, Environment in Address to World Economic Forum in Davos, UN Press Release SG/SM/6881.

[242] UN Secretary-General Kofi Annan to the United States Chamber of Commerce, in Washington, D.C., June 8, 1999, UN Press Release SG/SM/7022.

[243] Business Backs Trade Role for UN, *The Guardian,* July 6, 1999; and Businesses Promise UN Boss to be Good Citizens, *Reuters,* July 5, 1999, both cited in *Corporate Europe Observer,* Issue 5, October 1999.

[244] U.S. Chamber of Commerce website, http://www.uschamber.com.

[245] David Vogel, *Fluctuating Fortunes: The Political Power of Business in America* (Basic Books, 1989), p. 34.

[246] *Encyclopedia of Interest Groups and Lobbyists in the United States* (Sharpe, 2000), p. 117-119.

[247] Center for Responsive Politics, www.opensecrets.org.

[248] *Encyclopedia of Interest Groups and Lobbyists in the United States* (Sharpe, 2000), p. 117-119.

[249] *Encyclopedia of Interest Groups and Lobbyists in the United States* (Sharpe, 2000), p. 117-119.

[250] U.S. Chamber of Commerce, website, http://www.uschamber.com.

[251] U.S. Chamber of Commerce, website, http://www.uschamber.com.

[252] The NFIB, created in 1943, has 560,000 small-business members, but it too is controlled by a small board of the more conservative. The NFIB has a staff of 700 and a budget of $58 million — almost as much as the Chamber of Commerce. G. William Domhoff, *Who Rules America?: Power and Politics in the Year 2000* (Mayfield, 1998), p. 57.

[253] David Vogel, *Fluctuating Fortunes: The Political Power of Business in America* (Basic Books, 1989), p. 202, 253.

[254] U.S. Chamber of Commerce, website, http://www.uschamber.com.

[255] U.S. Chamber of Commerce, website, http://www.uschamber.com.

[256] U.S. Chamber of Commerce, website, http://www.uschamber.com.

[257] U.S. Chamber of Commerce, website, http://www.uschamber.com. The Center for Corporate Citizenship, 1615 H St. NW, Washington, DC 20062, telephone 202.463.5517, fax 202.463.5308.

[258] Center for International Private Enterprise (CIPE), 1155 15th Street NW #700, Washington DC 20005, telephone 202.721.9200, fax 202.721.9250, Web: http://www.cipe.org/.

[259] From ExIm Bank news releases, http://206.3.143.3/press/press.html.

[260] U.S. General Accounting Office, *U.S. Export-Import Bank: Issues Raised by Recent Market Developments and Foreign Competition*, U.S. GAO Testimony, Oct. 7, 1998, GAO/T-NSIAD-99-23.

[261] Amazon Watch, *Arteries for Global Trade* (1997), excerpted at ECA-Watch, http://www.eca-watch.org/artsivam.html. *See also* Todd Lewan, Charges of Corruption and Fraud Surround Amazon Radar Project, *Seattle Times,* Aug. 27, 1995, p. A19.

[262] Nicaragua Solidarity Network Of Greater New York, *Weekly News Update On The Americas*, Issue #526, Feb 27, 2000 and *Legal Times* (Washington, DC), Feb. 23, 2000, excerpted by ECA-Watch, http://www.eca-watch.org/arteximocci.html.

[263] William D. Hartung, *Welfare for Weapons Dealers 1998*, World Policy Institute Issue Brief, March 1998, http://worldpolicy.org/projects/arms/reports.html.

[264] Federal Reserve Bank, http://www.bog.frb.fed.us/bios/, January 17, 2000.

[265] Federal Reserve Bank, http://www.bog.frb.fed.us/bios/, January 17, 2000.

[266] Federal Reserve Bank, http://www.bog.frb.fed.us/bios/, January 17, 2000.

[267] Kevin Phillips, Headed for a Fall?, *Los Angeles Times,* January 16, 2000.

[268] OPIC 1991 Annual Report, p.30.

[269] OPIC website, http://www.opic.gov.

[270] OPIC news release, Feb 4, 2000.

[271] OPIC news release, Feb 29, 2000.

[272] OPIC news release, Feb 4, 2000.

273 Standard & Poor's, Political Risk Insurance May Enhance Emerging Market Structured Transactions, http://www.standardandpoor.com/ratings/structuredfinance/politicalrisk.htm.

274 OPIC news release, June 13, 2000.

275 OPIC news release, June 13, 2000.

276 OPIC news release, June 13, 2000.

277 OPIC news release, June 13, 2000.

278 OPIC news release, March 21, 2000.

279 OPIC news release, March 21, 2000.

280 http://www.usaengage.org/background/about.html, August 25, 2000.

281 http://www.usaengage.org/background/members.html, August 25, 2000.

282 http://www.usaengage.org/legislative/albrecht.html.

283 http://www.usaengage.org/news/kittredge2.html.

284 http://www.usaengage.org/legislative/lanetest1.html.

285 USA*Engage praised a U.S. House vote to ease the trade embargo against Cuba, http://www.usaengage.org/resources/release_072100.html and congratulated House and Senate Committees for agreeing to lift food and medicine sanctions against Cuba and a handful of other countries, http://www.usaengage.org/resources/cubamed_release.html.

286 Lori Wallach and Michelle Sforza, *Whose Trade Organization? Corporate Globalization and the Erosion of Democracy* (Public Citizen, 1999), p. 172, 188.

287 http://www.usaengage.org/supremecourt.html.

288 http://www.usaengage.org/background/lawsuit/amicuslist-nftc.html.

289 A map of state and local sanctions is at http://www.usaengage.org/resources/map3.html and analysis is at http://www.usaengage.org/news/status.html.

290 USA*Engage's news releases are at http://www.usaengage.org/news/991209pr.html and http://www.usaengage.org/resources/release_8_11_2000.htm and http://www.usaengage.org/resources/release_080100.html.

291 http://www.usaengage.org/resources/links.html.

292 Tom Athanasiou, *Divided Planet: The Ecology of Rich and Poor* (Little-Brown, 1996), p. 46.

293 See the IMF webpage, http://www.imf.org/external/np/exr/facts/surv.htm.

294 Cornerhouse, *Exporting Corruption: Privatisation, Multinationals and Bribery,* Cornerhouse Briefing 19, http://icaap.org/Cornerhouse/.

295 PrivatizationLink website, http://privatizationlink.ipanet.net/.

296 Cornerhouse, *Exporting Corruption: Privatisation, Multinationals and Bribery,* Cornerhouse Briefing 19, p. 11-12, http://icaap.org/Cornerhouse/.

297 The U.S., Japan, Germany, France, and the UK currently control 40 percent of the IMF votes, http://www.imf.org/external/np/sec/memdir/eds.htm.

298 IFC 1999 Annual Report, http://www.ifc.org/ar99/.

299 Rainforest Action Network, Case Study on Citibank and World Bank bonds, http://www.ran.org/ran_campaigns/citigroup/frame.start.html.

300 http://www.worldbank.org/ida/idao.html.

301 Schmidheiny has been a director of the engineering giant ABB (Asea Brown Boveri) and Nestle. He has been involved in the production of asbestos in Brazil and Costa Rica, and of steel in Chile. He is also the principal shareholder of Inversiones Suizandina, which controls Forestal Terranova S.A., one of the largest exporters of wood from the native forests of Chile. BCSD endorsed Aracruz Celulose, a huge eucalyptus pulp mill in Brazil, as an exemplar of sustainable development. Kenny Bruno and Jed Greer, *Greenpeace Book of Greenwash*, Greenpeace International, 1992.

302 http://www.bca.com.au/docs/19julyworld.htm and http://www.wbcsd.ch/whatis.htm#aims.

303 http://www.wbcsd.ch/memlist.htm#top.

304 http://www.wbcsd.ch/sectoral/forestry/index.htm.

305 http://www.weforum.org/aboutforum.nsf/Documents/Home+About+the+Forum.

306 Walden Bello, *From Melbourne to Prague: The Struggle for a Deglobalized World*, Talk delivered at a series of engagements on the occasion of demonstrations against the World Economic Forum (Davos) in Melbourne, Australia, 6-10 September 2000. http://focusweb.org/.

307 http://www.weforum.org/mediacenter.nsf/Documents/Home+-Media+Center+Forthcoming+Events.

308 *Europa Directory of International Organizations*, p. 451-452.

309 All from Lori Wallach and Michelle Sforza, *Whose Trade Organization? Corporate Globalization and the Erosion of Democracy* (Public Citizen, 1999).

310 Martin Khor, Letter Sent by 11 Countries to WTO Chair Criticising Green Room Process, Global Policy Forum, *News from Geneva*, Nov. 15, 1999, http://www.globalpolicy.org/socecon/bwi-wto/wto99/letter.htm. *See also* John Howard, Third World Says No To Green Room WTO Bullying, *Scoop Headlines*, Dec 5, 1999, http://www.scoop.co.nz/stories/HL9912/S00022.htm.

311 Center for Responsive Politics, http://www.opensecrets.org/pubs/lobby98/topspend.htm.

312 John R. MacArthur, *The Selling of "Free Trade": NAFTA, Washington, and the Subversion of American Democracy* (Hill And Wang, 2000), p. 168.

313 Center for Responsive Politics, http://www.opensecrets.org/pubs/lobby98/topoervall.htm.

314 Charles Lewis and the Center for Public Integrity, *The Buying of the President 2000*, (Avon, 2000), p. 53-574, 91-95.

315 Table compiled by Grattan Healy, http://ourworld.compuserve.com/homepages/grattan_healy/Bild-az-tab.html, August 14, 2000.

Be joyful though you have considered all the facts.

Wendell Berry

6665